RUNNING A SCHOOL
LIBRARY MEDIA CENTER
SECOND EDITION

A How-To-Do-It Manual
for Librarians

Barbara L. Stein
Risa W. Brown

HOW-TO-DO-IT MANUALS
FOR LIBRARIANS

NUMBER 121

NEAL-SCHUMAN PUBLISHERS, INC.
New York, London

Published by Neal-Schuman Publishers, Inc.
100 Varick Street
New York, NY 10013

Library of Congress Cataloging-in-Publication Data

Stein, Barbara L.
    Running a school library media center : a how-to-do-it manual /
Barbara L. Stein, Risa W. Brown. — 2nd ed.
        p. cm. — (How-do-do-it manuals for librarians ; #121)
    ISBN 1-55570-439-5 (alk. paper)
    1. School libraries—Administration—Handbooks, manuals, etc.
    2. Instructional materials centers—Administration—Handbooks,
manuals, etc. I. Brown, Risa W. II. Title. III. How-to-do-it manuals for
libraries ; no. 121.
    Z675.S3 S757 2002
    025.1'978—dc21

                                                                2002 002987

CONTENTS

LIST OF FIGURES

PREFACE

Managing today's school library media center is a complicated and demanding task. Technology has made the school library media center seem like a completely different environment from the libraries of the past, but many of the basic premises hold true. The school library media center's mission—its *raison d'etre*—remains the same as it was fifty years ago.

Our users expect us to have many skills. We have always been and still are expected to be service-oriented when dealing with students and staff, knowledgeable about materials, and comfortable as budgeters and space planners. Added to that, today's school library media specialists must be knowledgeable of Internet sources, confident in the knowledge of computer applications, and undaunted by mastering new information formats such as database research and interactive video. Today's librarian must comfortably wear many hats, and change them easily.

This updated and expanded edition of *Running a School Library Media Center: A How-To-Do-It Manual* offers a starting-from-scratch introduction to library media specialists who are just starting their first jobs; more experienced library professionals, paraprofessionals, and clerks will also find information and resources of value in these pages

The library media specialist's job is demanding. Wearing all of the required hats is both rewarding and overwhelming. It requires knowledge of library technical and management skills, as well as good public relations and sound educational practices. Chapter 1 offers survival strategies including goal setting, time management, and stress management to help you perform at your best. Chapter 2 examines the major administrative aspects of running a school library, such as writing policies and procedures, scheduling, budgeting, and preparing reports. Collection development and technical services are considered next: How are materials selected? What selection tools do you need? How do you order materials? What do you do when materials arrive to prepare them for use? How do you circulate, inventory, weed, and discard materials? What do you do when materials are challenged? Chapters 3 through 6 systematically tackle these questions for both books and for other materials (such as periodicals, vertical files, audiovisuals, and equipment). Chapter 3 discusses procedures for ordering and processing materials. Chapter 4 concerns cataloging, Chapter 5 covers circulation, and Chapter 6 deals with maintaining the collection.

Staff duties are outlined in Chapter 7. How do you train new support staff, student assistants, and volunteers? This chapter contains advice on interviewing and hiring staff, what to look for and what you may or may not ask, as well as sample job descriptions. Chapter 8 is devoted to the physical facility with particular attention to ways you arrange your facility to gain the most effective use of space.

Chapter 9 deals with information literacy. What skills do today's students need in an information rich environment? How do you plan research projects that will encourage the development of those skills? How do you create a partnership with the other educational professionals in your school? Chapter 9 offers practical suggestions to help you with this aspect of your position. Chapter 10 covers all aspects of programming in your media center. Hints are provided for special events such as author visits, storytelling, booktalks, book fairs, RIF (Reading Is Fundamental) distributions, and providing other services to teachers, the administration, and students. Chapter 10 covers ways you can promote your media center.

The appendixes are a valuable part of this book. While many of the sources are referred to in the text itself, the appendixes are a time-saving ready reference for quick referral. They include book, periodical, and AV vendors; sources for supplies, book and AV reviews, free and inexpensive materials and instructional aids; a learning style indicator, professional associations, and the Library Bill of Rights. The Library Evaluator is a tool that was developed in the Houston Independent School District (ISD) to systematically evaluate every aspect of the library program in accordance with the Texas Education Association guidelines known as TEKS. It can be a powerful way to measure your needs, help you develop your vision and communicate that vision with your principal. This evaluation tool is available at *www.school-library.org* with the calculations keyed in. All you need to do is put an X in the appropriate box and the percentages are automatically calculated. It was developed by the Houston Area Librarians with special efforts by: Kellie Skarda, secretary to Sarah Wahl, library coordinator at Goose Creed CISD; Karen Flavin, Library Coordinator, Alief ISD; and Evelyn Beyer, Technology Teacher, Stafford High School.

When we set out to update and revise *Running a School Library Media Center*, we looked at what readers told us they most valued from the first edition. Without a doubt, the most popular feature were forms, schedules, and checklists which readers could adapt to their own specific situations. Thus, we've sought to provide in this revision even more of these so that this volume essentially provides a ready reference for the routine and clerical matters that take up much of any librarian's time. We hope our practical approach taken here will help free professionals to perform the teaching and programming functions that are the primary task of a library media specialist.

ACKNOWLEDGMENTS

It is impossible to name all of those who contribute to an understanding of the school library profession. Every book and article read, every workshop or conference attended, every discussion with colleagues, and every class taught, helped to shape our ideas and presentation of this material.

Special appreciation is extended to the following people for their assistance with the preparation of *Running a School Library Media Center*. Yunfe Du cheerfully provided expert technical assistance. Several school districts influenced the contents. School library media specialists and district directors freely shared ideas, forms, and suggestions. Thelma Gay, library director of the Richardson Independent School District, supplied many materials, as did several library vendors such as Brodart and EBSCO. A special thank you is due to Chris Salerno of Carrollton-Farmers Branch ISD and to Houston area librarians.

We appreciate the patience of our colleagues and families, and the insights from Dr. Robert Martin.

RUNNING A SCHOOL
LIBRARY MEDIA CENTER

1 GETTING STARTED

Congratulations! You are now a library media specialist. Now what? As you look around your library, you feel a sense of panic as well as pride. What do you do first? What is expected of you?

Information Power: Building Partnerships for Learning (ALA, 1998) defines the role of the school library media specialist as "the essential link who connects students, teachers and others with the information resources they need . . . [using] collaboration, technology and leadership" (ALA, 1998: 4). This definition reflects the growing emphasis on the information skills role that the school library media program plays in achieving these goals. *Information Power* was prepared by a committee made up of members of the American Association of School Librarians (AASL) and the Association for Educational Communication and Technology (AECT) and provides guidelines on all aspects of running a school library media program. It has become a standard document for all school libraries.

Library media specialists have much more to do than you might have first realized, and if this is a new job for you, you are probably overwhelmed. Relax. Take a few days to explore your new surroundings. Find out about the procedures already in place. Look for an aide, a volunteer, an administrator, or a teacher who can brief you on various aspects of library operating procedures in the past year. If everyone is satisfied with the procedures, allow operations to remain in place for now.

Look through the files for written records of past events and a procedures manual. If procedures are not written down, begin gathering materials for a policies and procedures manual. As you compile the manual and wish to make changes, make them slowly. Gradual changes will be less threatening than abrupt ones to the staff and to the media center users and will enhance your image.

Once you have a familiarity with basic procedures, learn about the people in your school environment, the library facility, and the collection.

> Learn as much as you can quickly, but make changes slowly.

THE PEOPLE

The people in your school are your target audience (clientele) and will create your most challenging situations. The building principal is the educational leader of the school and his concept of the media center and its role in that school is central to what you do and your success in doing it. Try to discover what the building principal expects from the media program. Other teachers, administrators, and media staff can add their perceptions to whatever signals you get from your principal. Everyone—audiovisual administrators, the media center staff, teachers, and students—will inform, impact, and inspire your development of the library media program.

The media center staff includes clerks, aides, student assistants, and volunteers. What does each person on the staff view as her duties? Are there any written job descriptions? How have tasks been previously assigned? What is the hierarchy of authority among aides, student assistants, and volunteers?

Teachers use the library as a resource for both their students and themselves. Their present use can give you a starting point for development as well as clues about the media center's adequacy. Find out how teachers use the media center for teaching and how materials available in the library help them. Do teachers use library materials themselves? Find out how teachers use online resources. Information resources have changed tremendously in the last several years. Is everyone comfortable using the new resources? Are the databases and subscriptions the best for the needs of the staff?

Student use will also reveal needs. How are students admitted to the media center? When are students allowed to come to the media center? Is the schedule rigid or flexible? What are the rules and regulations students are expected to observe? Do they understand the rules?

Your library colleagues in the district and local area are an invaluable source of information about district policies, shared databases, suggested lesson plans, even insights on the operation before you arrived. They are also going through the process of "setting up" for another year. Don't be afraid to draw on their expertise and experience.

Who are the people?
• administrators
• media center staff
• teachers
• students

THE FACILITY

Locate major landmarks and observe the arrangement of space. Although the physical features of a facility cannot be readily changed, you should be aware of how these features affect the overall library program. You might be able to change some aspects of the space to accommodate your program.

The way in which classes come to the library is affected by the

Figure 1–1 Equipment Control Chart				
Media Center	Repair	Room 6	Room 12	Room 18
Boom Box	Room 1	Room 7	Room 13	Room 19
VCR	Room 2	Room 8	Room 14	Room 20
Laser Disc	Room 3	Room 9	Room 15	Room 21
Video Camera	Room 4	Room 10	Room 16	Room 22
Overhead	Room 5	Room 11	Room 17	Room 23

location of the media center. Is the library media center centrally located? Do students and faculty have easy access to the entire facility? If not, potential users might be discouraged from using the library.

The arrangement of furniture and shelving has a direct impact on the library operation. Does the arrangement provide for smooth traffic patterns? Is there enough room for the computers and related hardware? Is there a work area close to the reference section? Is there comfortable seating near the current periodicals and newspapers? Each major function, such as reference and circulation, should have enough space. Is there a class area and an independent study area that can be used simultaneously? Is the reference section too close to another highly used section? Is the circulation desk located close to the door for good control and security? Is there undesirable traffic through the library for any reason?

Your facility design and layout directly affect equipment distribution and media use. Where is the equipment stored? Is it easily available for distribution to classrooms? As it is helpful to know where equipment is at a glance, you could benefit from an equipment control chart (see Figure 1–1). If one does not exist, you might want to make one (Chapter 5 explains how). Also, where are the audiovisual media stored? Are these media mixed in with other materials or housed in a separate area? Is there equipment set up in the library center for use of audiovisual materials?

Learn how the circulation system works. Even if there is a staff in place to do the routine tasks, learn it yourself and get comfortable enough with its operation so you can handle circulation tasks with ease. Make cheat sheets if necessary until the commands become second nature or for future reference if the operation is an occasional one.

Finally, good signage will help media center users become more efficient and independent in using the center. Is the label signage adequate? Are there instructions for using the available online resources? Are the rules for behavior in the library posted?

THE COLLECTION

Determine what is in the collection and what is needed to support the present curriculum. As you examine the collection, note copyright and release dates and balance in relation to curriculum areas. Be especially sensitive to the age of the reference materials. Eventually, you will need to know the curriculum thoroughly in order to determine whether the collection meets the school's needs. Try to obtain the curriculum guides from which teachers work. Look for titles listed in professional bibliographies and those in current textbooks. Observe which new books are most used. What subjects are checked out? For how long are books checked out?

Familiarize yourself with the online databases and other online resources that the district provides or to which the school already subscribes. Everyone will expect you to be able to show them how to use these tools. Even databases that have been in place for many years can require a refresher course so teachers and students will see their usefulness. While patrons are quick to turn to the Internet for information needs, subscription services can often yield better information more quickly and the information is more reliable. Prepare demonstrations and incorporate them into orientations.

GOAL SETTING

If you are a library media specialist in a new situation, you might feel you do not yet know enough to set goals and objectives. Activities and even objectives could change as you become familiar with a school. However, you need goals to guide your program's direction. Start with a list of broad goals. Determine objectives for each goal, set priorities, plan activities, and then evaluate them. Write down steps toward each objective.

Begin with a list of broad goals such as: 1) selecting, acquiring, and organizing materials to support the educational process; 2) instructing students on the use of materials; 3) planning for use of materials; 4) expanding and promoting the use of the media center by students, teachers, and the administration.

Once you have broad goals firmly in mind, you can write objectives. At this point, do not set your goals so high that you cannot possibly achieve them. Write down your goal and the activity you plan to use, then give yourself a time frame and evaluate. A typical program plan might look like the following example:

> **Objective:** Help teachers learn enough about media center materials and services so they feel confident in making individualized resource, library-based assignments for students.
>
> **Priority step:** Focus on helping new teachers use media center materials and services.
>
> **Activity:** Invite new teachers to a "Get Acquainted" luncheon in the library. While they are in the library, explain various services and offer your help.
>
> **Plan of action:** Before the school year starts, check the inservice training schedule and try to get a session for library services included on it. Be sure the principal allows you time to address teachers, and try to get a commitment of release time for teachers to attend. Plan and schedule workshops to acquaint new teachers with media center services and materials.
>
> **Evaluation:** Jot down notes about the results of your activities so you can evaluate them later. Did teachers attend workshops? Did they request information about materials and services? Are they willing to involve you in curriculum planning?

As you form your goals and objectives, be sure to base them on the goals, policies, and philosophies of the school and district.

A Program Plan Needs:

- broad goals
- objectives
- priorities
- planned activities
- evaluation procedures

Become familiar with school district policy, state education policy or guidelines, school improvement plans, the faculty handbook, the student handbook, and previous years' media center records and reports.

You might be required to turn in a formal list of goals and objectives for your program. Even if you are not required to do so, give these to your principal as well as a brief description of your plans for your program. When your administrator understands what you are trying to accomplish, you are much more likely to receive the full support you need.

SIX ESSENTIAL SURVIVAL STRATEGIES

Utilizing the following six strategies in your day-to-day work will help preserve your sanity and facilitate your ability to effectively serve your school.

1. **Achieve more with less stress.** First, don't panic. Second, plan. Once tasks are broken down into small, easily achievable steps, you will see things get done before your eyes.
2. **Develop, update, maintain, and use a policy/procedures manual.** Make sure there is a policy and procedures manual so you don't have to waste time on a policy decision for each situation. In addition, train the staff to know the policy so they can enforce it with minimal involvement from you.
3. **Set goals.** Maintain your list of goals. Once you know your goals, set priorities for each of them and work on the most important goals first.
4. **List objectives for each goal.** Make a list of steps required to fulfill each objective, establish a plan of action, and transfer necessary information to your calendar. Make a "To Do" list a habit and make it every day at the same time. Keep a "Bring Up" file with dates ahead for each month.
5. **Don't procrastinate.** Do the jobs you dislike the most first. Use every bit of time for something worthwhile. For instance, if you must remain at the circulation desk during lunch, find another task to do at the same time such as opening mail, reading reviews, and so on.
6. **File it or throw it.** Handle items only once. As soon as you look at them, decide whether you are going to keep circulars, memos, correspondence, catalogs, and so forth. Then deal with each item: file it, answer it, or throw it away.

Time is wasted by repeatedly looking at items. Keep your environment as organized and clutter free as possible. If you find yourself wasting valuable time looking for things, that's a signal to organize.

STRESS MANAGEMENT

Stress reduction strategies will help you maintain a positive attitude and avoid burnout. There are a variety of methods, both internal and external, you can use to help you adjust to your environment so you can handle your daily stress. Internal exercises will keep your attitude healthy. Here are some general tips for internal stress management:

- *Be flexible*. Be willing to look at your established patterns, programs, or procedures with an eye for improvement.
- *Find a way to relax*. For some, deep breathing or meditation works. Others keep a picture of a beach or the mountains and visualize themselves there. Practice relaxing often.
- *Don't berate yourself*. If there is something you dislike about yourself, visualize yourself handling a situation in a way you perceive as more desirable. If you find it hard to say "no," practice saying no in many ways until you find a way that suits you.
- *Enjoy your work*. Rather than dread the chores, look forward to the joys.

External stress management incorporates those around you. These signals will help you become a stronger part of your community. Here are some general tips for external stress management:

- *Anticipate stressful situations and plan your response to them*. Know the steps you would take to resolve any conflict: an irate parent's complaint about a book, a disruptive student, being called to the principal's office, for example.
- *Be professional*. Attend workshops, take classes, read professional literature, and so on. Set professional goals for yourself to grow into.
- *Respect other faculty*. Usually that respect will be returned.
- *Nurture the students*. Good relationships with students are quite rewarding.

Find someone in the school with whom you can talk. Inform everyone what your role is in the school community. You are not a baby-sitter nor are you presiding over a "frill" service; you are a core part of the school's instructional team.

Become involved in any change as it is being planned. If you have input into changes, such as remodeling, you can contribute working solutions to problems before they develop. Lobby for far-reaching changes on the local, state, even national levels.

PROFESSIONAL ORGANIZATIONS

You need to receive information, ideas, and reinforcement from other people in your profession. The key to a profession is its organizations. Journals, periodicals, and newsletters help you stay informed about changes and challenges in the profession. Meetings and conferences put you in contact with people who will share ideas with you. Attending a conference can stimulate your energy and enthusiasm levels and give you ideas and solutions.

Many professional organizations, libraries, and school districts maintain excellent Web pages filled with useful information and links to other sites. These can provide excellent teaching plans and ideas for activities as well as professional readings. In addition, there are library- and school-related listservs to which you can subscribe. Then postings will come to you about different current concerns.

There are many associations from which you can choose. These include library, audiovisual, and teacher organizations at the local, state, national, and international levels. You might consider the following professional organizations or consult the broader listing in Appendix L.

1. American Library Association (ALA): As a member you will receive the journal *American Libraries*. The annual conference is attended by suppliers, vendors, and library service providers and offers programs that will keep you up to date and knowledgeable about your field. The divisions of greatest importance to you are the American Association for School Librarians (membership entitles you to receive *Knowledge Quest*), the Association for Library Service to Children, and the Young Adult Library Services Association. Members in the latter two divisions also receive *Journal of Youth Services in Libraries*.

2. Your state library association or state school library or educational media association if it is separate.
3. National Education Association (NEA) or American Federation of Teachers (AFT).
4. Your state and local affiliates of NEA or AFT.
5. Other related organizations: International Reading Association, Phi Delta Kappa, National Council of Teachers of English, Association of Supervision and Curriculum Development.

2 POLICIES AND PROCEDURES

DO YOU REALLY NEED A WRITTEN POLICY?

Yes! A written policy establishes guidelines for the smooth operation of the media center even in your absence and provides authority and protection for you and your staff when problems arise. Every library media specialist has a philosophy and a policy under which to operate, whether it is written or not. The value of a written policy is that the people around you know what the center's policy is and can help you enforce it. In addition, once the written policy is approved by your administration, you can carry it out with confidence.

To be most effective, your written policy should incorporate the philosophy of the school district and state your library's own mission. It should specify who is responsible for selection of materials, including which major selection tools are used. Make your decisions about circulation policies, then formalize them in your policy and procedures manual. Decide on how to evaluate gifts. Set a procedure for handling challenges, criticism, or attempts to censor materials (including electronic ones).

Involve the staff in writing the policy and procedures manual. Not only will this help you get started, but your staff will see if improvements can be made as they outline their established patterns. They will be receptive to changes that they help formulate.

INTERNET USE AND OTHER COMPUTER-RELATED POLICIES

An important part of your policy will be your rules governing Internet access, use, and consequences of violations. If possible, write your policy and procedures before you introduce Internet services, which means you will need to draw on the experiences of other librarians, published guides, and the expertise of other experts. If you come into a situation where Internet use is already in place, thoroughly understand the policy knowing that you will be the one enforcing it. Another decision you might have to make is to filter or not to filter, although frequently this is a districtwide decision. There is a list of filtering products in Appendix J.

Some decisions that you need to make before students get online are: Can students get into chat rooms; can students check their e-

> **TIP:** To inform parents of your Internet policies and procedures and to answer technology-related questions, make a presentation at a PTA meeting or plan a presentation at Open House.

TIP: Post a list of specific consequences for specific violations of your Internet policy.

mail; do you limit how long a student can use the computers; will you allow printing services; and can students use a floppy disk, zip disk, or their own CD? Then you must decide how to handle unacceptable uses of the school's Internet facilities: illegal activities, commercial activity, damaging machines, ruining someone else's data, sending or posting hate messages, gaining unauthorized access to unacceptable online resources, using someone else's account, accessing obscene materials and downloading it, and bypassing the filtering system. Some violations might only require demerits, warnings, or other forms of disciplinary action; other violations could result in revoking a student's Internet use privilege.

Once your written policy is established, consider placing it on the school or library Web page if there is one. If any policy questions arise, you or your patrons can access the policy quickly and easily. Since the Internet is a relatively new aspect of the library policy, decide on a method of communication with parents that will inform them of the expectations and drawbacks of their student using the Internet. Most districts have instituted a permission form based on their Internet policy and have the parents sign a form before allowing students access to the Internet (see Figure 2–1).

WHEN IS THE MEDIA CENTER OPEN?

Consider keeping your media center open longer than the school day. *Information Power* states that the media center is to be available outside of class time, including hours before and after school, evenings, Saturday mornings, and summer. Extended scheduling helps many students by giving them access to both print and online resources they might not have otherwise. With the growing popularity of "Extended Day" activities, there are more opportunities to extend library hours as well.

Some factors that can discourage extended hours are staffing and your school's policy on building use outside of school hours. If you have a small staff, you will have difficulty covering more hours; it is difficult for one person to keep the library open during school hours as well as before and after school. If you ask the staff to help you with extended hours, make arrangements for them to receive compensatory time. Part-time help can be scheduled to arrive early or stay late. You might be able to stagger the

Figure 2–1 Internet Permission Form

STUDENT AGREEMENT and APPLICATION
FOR RISD ELECTRONIC COMMUNICATION AND DATA MANAGEMENT SYSTEM ACCESS

APPLICATION

Student Full Name (Please print) _____

Student I.D. Number (accounts cannot be issued without this)_____

Current Grade _____ Current School_____

Student Home Address _____

Student Home Phone _____

When the account is established, the teacher will notify user of log-on name and user password.

Employee Full Name _____

Position/Assignment _____

AGREEMENT

STUDENT - I have read and understand the Electronic Communication and Data Management Acceptable Use Plan (AUP) for the RISD and I agree to abide by the AUP as a condition of access to the District's electronic communication and data management systems, including the Internet and Intranet. I further understand and agree that if I violate the AUP, I will be subject to appropriate disciplinary action and revocation or limitation of system access. Any illegal conduct may be reported to the appropriate authorities.

Student Signature_____

Date_____

PARENT OR GUARDIAN — If the applicant is under the age of 18, a parent or guardian must read and sign this agreement.
As the parent or guardian of this student, I have read and understand the Acceptable Use Plan for the RISD. I hereby authorize RISD to issue an account for my child with Limited or Full access as indicated below and certify that the information contained on this form is correct.

_____ No Internet access or privileges (Limited Access)
_____ Internet access and privileges (Full Access)

Parent or Guardian (Please print) _____

Signature _____ Date _____

Daytime Phone Number _____ Evening Phone Number_____

Used with permission of the Richardson Independent School District

TIP: If you cannot accommodate the full schedule Information Power suggests, try at least to be open before and after school and certainly during lunch.

schedules so that the person who opens leaves early and the person who stays after arrives later.

If school or district policy discourages use of the building during extended hours, work with administrators to develop a system allowing students use of the library. This could be accomplished with passes issued the day before by you or the teacher.

HOW DO YOU SCHEDULE CLASSES?

There are different ways of scheduling student and teacher use of the media center. *Information Power* recommends that you keep your schedule as flexible as possible, giving users the widest possible access: "Any functions that restrict or interfere with open access to all resources including scheduled classes on a fixed basis, must be avoided to the fullest extent possible." You might need to use a combination of two or more of the following types of schedules to devise the best system for your teachers and students.

1. **Flexible scheduling** allows for voluntary use of the library whenever needed by teachers and students. As you become increasingly involved in the instructional process, flexible scheduling allows you to expand and enhance the work of classroom and textbook because the media center will be more available to small groups and individuals for independent study and research.
2. **Fixed scheduling** means classes are assigned to use the library at a specified time every week. Users are ensured library time. Early childhood and kindergarten classes and reading classes benefit from this structured kind of scheduling.
3. **Block time scheduling** allows teachers to reserve a block of time for library use; for example, a class might use the library for a week at a time for a project or reserve a period for book selection.
4. **Open scheduling** means classes have no scheduled time. Individual students and classes are allowed to come or be sent to the library whenever they need to use its resources.

A lesson plan book (either print or electronic) is one way to communicate to teachers that you plan for their classes as much

TIP: You can use an electronic planner to schedule classes if your district is networked. This is an easy way for everyone to see when and how much the library is used. Be sure you follow up with the teacher for planning purposes with e-mail or a face-to-face visit.

What factors influence scheduling?
- size of the media center staff
- size of the media center facility
- size of each class

TIP: Be sure to include the scheduling policy in your written procedures, after it is arrived at in consultation with teachers, the administration, and your own staff.

as they do. Let teachers know that they not only reserve a spot for their class (which lets other teachers know that the space is being used), but they are reserving your time and expertise. This point of contact is a good time to consult with the teacher about his lesson and offer to help plan it.

You might also find yourself responsible for scheduling an adjacent computer lab. You can use your master plan book to schedule the lab so you will be aware of traffic through the library. If you are in any way responsible for lessons that occur there, you will want to include it on your calendar. You might wish to distance yourself from the computer lab operation. Set up a schedule for the lab and put it in a convenient location.

Try to avoid situations where the teacher leaves her class with you. Discourage your principal from putting you into the "rotation" so that library becomes an activity period. Similarly, have your principal emphasize to teachers the need for them to stay with their classes. Your goal is to work as a team member with your teacher colleagues and together carry out lesson plans and activities.

The size of your library and other factors will play into decisions about scheduling techniques. The size of the media center staff is directly related to the time available to the media specialist for instruction. Too many students overwhelm a small staff. There might be room for only one class at a time. Larger classes will take longer to complete a unit.

BUDGETS

Library media specialists are responsible for handling the financial transactions of the library media center. This involves accountability for large expenditures of funds allocated by the district. Each school and school district has its own system for budget control.

Find out how budgets are handled at your school. Find out how to submit a budget proposal and follow district and school policy guidelines. Try not to be intimidated by budgeting: It is part of your job.

If your district has a centralized media services director, that person can help you with the accepted format. Check with your principal or administrator in your building who is responsible for the budget. Ask questions!

Plan your budget around your goals. Knowing the requirements

Figure 2–2 Sample Line-Item Budget					
Account number	Line Item	Last Year	This Year	Next Year	Reason
303.101	Books	$3,000	$4,000	$6,000	To keep the collection up to date and expand geography, cultural affairs, and multicultural holdings.
303.102	Periodicals Newspapers	400	500	600	To cover inflation.
303.103	Online Subscriptions	0	2,000	4,000	To subscribe to an online periodical database.
303.104	Nonprint Materials A.V. Software Computer Software	3,000	6,000	4,000	To add videos and computer software to achieve state media standards.
303.105	Binding	100	100	150	To repair worn books.
303.106	Supplies	150	150	150	To cover increases in computer-related supplies.
303.107	Furniture	500	1,000	900	To add computer workstations.
303.108	Equipment	500	500	3,000	To add computers.
303.109	Equipment Repair	50	50	250	To keep up with increased costs; includes preventative maintenance on VCRs and computers.
303.110	Memberships	50	50	50	To pay state dues.
303.111	Conferences	300	300	500	To attend state conference.

for the program as exactly as possible helps in justifying requests for money. You are asking for things that your program really needs because you have planned carefully. Show the specific ways in which required materials and equipment will be used to advance your programs. Usage statistics are an excellent way to show needs. Check to see if your circulation system maintains the statistics you need to back up your position.

If you have related state or regional accreditation standards and national guidelines to your goals and objectives, they can provide the best justification for anything you request. Standards are available from state education agency Web pages.

In some districts, you might not be required to submit a proposal or a formal justification for moneys spent, but go ahead and write them anyway and share them with your principal. This will help you evaluate your goals and plan of action, and it will help the administration to understand and appreciate the value of the library media program to teaching and learning.

TYPES OF BUDGETS

The main budget methods used in school libraries are line item and lump sum. In some situations funds can be drawn upon as needed; in others, all at one time; and in others, only at stated periodic dates.

Many organizations use a *line-item budget*, which simply assigns sums of money to broad categories such as periodicals or books. Line-item budgets are easy to prepare by taking amounts allocated for one year and adding anticipated cost increases. However, the past year's budget does not automatically fit a newly planned program. If, for example, you need different categories of items from one budget year to the next, you might have difficulty getting new allocations approved.

The *lump-sum budget* is also common. The media center might get all of its money in a lump sum without categorization. Then you must decide how to spend the money so your program gets what it needs. The problem with this system is that the program is planned according to the budget, rather than the budget being planned according to the program.

Even though a line-item list is not required, you might find that format valuable for planning if you are presented with a lump-sum budget. You can decide how much to spend on books, periodicals, audiovisuals, materials, supplies, and so on. If you need to focus on a database subscription in a particular year, you can more easily plan your budget around your needs. However, plan carefully so you get everything you need. If you spend your entire budget on one item, you neglect materials that need to be updated every year.

Keep good records of plans and expenditures so you can use them when planning the next year's budget. Once you go through the process, you will be able to develop short-term and long-term plans.

BUDGET RECORDS

You can use either a handwritten budget summary record to keep track of your budget or an electronic spreadsheet. You will need a record of the items that are paid for or canceled so you can tell how much money you have at any given time. There are com-

Figure 2–3 Sample Budget Summary Record

Account Number 303.101

Date	Description	deposits	expenses	balance
1/15/02	beginning balance	25,000.00		25,000.00
1/25/02	Baker & Taylor (PO #3523)		3,000.00	22,000.00
1/30/02	Bowker (PO #3539)		500.00	21,500.00
2/5/02	Perma Bound (PO #3553)		250.00	21,250.00
2/10/02	Gale (PO #3567)		250.00	21,000.00
2/15/02	EBSCO (PO #3580)		650.00	20,350.00
2/25/02	Wilson (PO #3597)		750.00	19,600.00
3/10/02	Highsmith (PO #3620)		175.00	19,425.00
				19,425.00

puter programs that will deduct the exact amounts paid out of your budget once you have entered the data. If someone calls on the phone or needs immediate information, you have that valuable information just a click away.

GRANTS AND PROPOSALS

You might want to expand your services by increasing technology or some other specific need that can be funded by outside sources. Experts say you must have a specific project that will result in learning. Donors want assurances that their dollars will make a difference. Be articulate and passionate.

Do your homework on the requirements for each grant. Some are for specific subject areas, types of material, or geographic region.

You will need to state the specific need and justify that need for the purposes of the grant application. You will have to state a plan of action and a process of evaluation. Recordkeeping is a must, both for justification and for evaluation. Statistics are a helpful part of this process.

Ask for help from those who have successfully received grant money. They will know what language to use and can advise you on how to shape a fundable project. There are also Web sites that provide information. The Foundation Center has advice and guidelines about funders: *www.fdcenter.org.*

Figure 2–4 Annual Library Media Center Report

Richardson Independent School District

School _____ Library Media Specialist _____ Year _____

  Enrollment _____   Number of classroom teachers _____

I. Adjusted Budget
    6669   Books   _____
    6394   Media   _____
    6398   Supplies   _____
    6329   Periodicals   _____
    6329   Bindery Services   _____   Total _____
  ____   _____   _____

II. Additional Budget

		Funded by Principal	Not Funded by Principal
_____	Travel	_____	_____
_____	Training	_____	_____
_____	Equipment Repair	_____	_____
_____	Bulbs	_____	_____
_____	Other	_____	_____
_____	Other	_____	_____
_____	Other	_____	_____
Totals:			

III.   Library Student Fund _____
        Balance as of _____ : _____ . Identify funding sources: PTA _____ Book Fair _____

IV. Library Media Center Collection

Volumes Added	_____	Volumes Withdrawn	_____
Media Added	_____	Media Withdrawn	_____
Items with Status of Lost	_____	Items with Status of Missing	_____
Total Volumes	_____	Volumes Per Student	_____
Total Media	_____	Media Per Student	_____
Total Periodicals	_____		_____
	_____		_____

Texas State Library Standards: (Identify ratings)
_____
_____

Circulation of Audiovisual Materials	_____	Circulation of Reference _____
Circulation of Books	_____	Circulation of Vertical File _____
Circulation of Periodicals	_____	Circulation of Equipment _____
Inter/Intra Library Loan: Loaned	_____	Borrowed _____

Number of Classes Scheduled During Year _____
Number of Classes Taught by Library Media Specialist
     (Include instruction carried out in classroom and Library Media Center _____

Figure 2–4 Continued

Student Assistants _____
Volunteers _____   Total Volunteer Hours _____

VI. Library Media Center Programs
     New Teacher Orientation   Date _____   Texas Library Association Promotion _____
     Student Orientation   Date _____   (Bluebonnet, Lone Star, Tayshas)
     Reading Promotion   Date _____
     Identify Activities:

     _____
     _____
     _____
     _____
     _____

     Staff Training   Date _____
     Identify Activities:

     _____
     _____
     _____
     _____
     _____

     Storytime   Date _____
     Author/Illustrator/Storyteller   Date _____

     _____
     _____
     _____
     _____
     _____

     Training/Seminars Attended (Outside district)
     Special Programs/Activities

     _____
     _____
     _____
     _____
     _____
     _____

REPORTS

Find out what reports your school and district require you to make during the year. Usually reports are statistics oriented, especially related to budgets and inventory.

Reports you might have to make include: a report to administration outlining attainment of goals and objectives; a report to

Figure 2–5 Automated Circulation Report

LHHS ANNUAL
YEARLY CIRCULATION REPORT
BRANCH - - Lake Highlands H.S.

01 AUG 2000 - 31 JUL 2001
Overview

	01 AUG 2000 -31 JUL 2001	01 AUG 1999 -31 JUL 2000	% Change
First Time Checkouts	4825	5793	−16.7%
Phone Renewals	4	3	33.3%
Self Renewals	0	0	0.0%
Renewals	263	335	−21.5%
ITEMS CHECKED OUT	5092	6131	−16.9%
Regular Checkins	5206	5201	0.1%
Late Checkins	1422	1974	−28.0%
ITEMS CHECKED IN	6628	7175	−7.6%

TIP: Find out before the first item is checked out if your circulation system maintains statistics and if they are available anytime during the year. Then you can decide if you need to keep an informal tally of any statistics such as materials added or withdrawn.

school or district on the number of materials in your collection by subject and format; a report on materials purchased with outside sources such as state or federal funds (this sometimes requires a special form); a report to school or district giving circulation statistics for the year, by months and subjects used.

There are a variety of methods to keep your circulation statistics. Check to see if your automated system keeps those statistics for you (see Figure 2–5). If not, then use a manual method. You can simply record the number and type of books checked out on a ledger or calendar with tally marks representing them. Using a ledger allows you to summarize each month, which makes an end-of-year report relatively easy to do.

Even if you are not required to make an annual report to the principal describing the progress of your program, do so if at all possible. Writing a report is a good opportunity to reflect and evaluate how well you achieved the goals set at the beginning of the year. This is a chance to present long-range plans and to solicit your principal's support.

Your annual report does not have to be long, but be sure to include purchases, inventory (the total collection including additions as well as losses and withdrawals), media center use (class use is important), and areas for improvement (where you can go from here. Be sure to emphasize the contributions you and the

Figure 2–6 Automated Collection Report

HIGH SCHOOL
Cataloging Additions and Deletions
BRANCH - Lake Highlands H.S.

01 AUG 2000 - 31 MAY 2001

Item Types

	Titles Added	Titles Deleted	Holdings Added	Holdings Deleted
High AV	233	18	308	35
High Book	1303	433	1372	652
High Paperback	44	7	48	8
High Periodicals				
High Reference	42	15	115	21
High Special Collect	4	0	4	0
High Vertical Files	0	1		
High Vertical Files				
HIGH SCHOOL TOTALS	1626	474	1847	716
High Equip - 1 Day	6	3	11	7
High Equip - 3 Day				
High Equip - Weekly	7	0	7	0
High Equip - Yearly	0	0	16	6
HIGH SCHOOL EQUIPMENT	13	3	34	13

library media program make to educational achievement and any specific school goals.

OTHER COMMUNICATIONS

E-mail is the most convenient form of communication with administration and teachers. There are still times that you might wish or be forced to issue memos in print form. Whatever the format, the rules for effective communication still apply:

- Spelling counts!
- Keep your writing succinct and to the point.
- Avoid flowery passages, long descriptive details, or emotional appeals.
- Be direct.

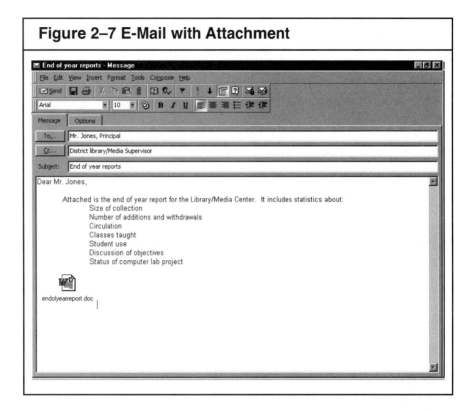

Figure 2–7 E-Mail with Attachment

End of year reports - Message

File Edit View Insert Format Tools Compose Help

Send

Arial | 10 | B I U

Message | Options

To... | Mr. Jones, Principal

Cc... | District library/Media Supervisor

Subject: | End of year reports

Dear Mr. Jones,

Attached is the end of year report for the Library/Media Center. It includes statistics about:
Size of collection
Number of additions and withdrawals
Circulation
Classes taught
Student use
Discussion of objectives
Status of computer lab project

endofyearreport.doc

YOUR PRINCIPAL

Communication with your principal is essential, and budget reports and statistics are just the beginning. *Information Power* states that "teachers, principals and teacher-librarians must form a partnership and plan together to design and implement the program that best matches the instructional needs of the school." It is imperative that your principal sees clearly the role of the librarian as well as that of the library program in the context of the entire school program. Libraries have undergone tremendous change in the last two decades, but principals might not be aware of the extent of the transitions. If they do not know what you are supposed to do, how will they know if you do it or make conditions best for you to do your job?

As a new person, it might be difficult finding out your principal's perception of your position before you find yourself in a tricky situation. You might find it awkward giving him the *Information Power* video for principals or articles that summarize the library's role in the school environment. Time might not permit frequent sit-down chats with your principal, but you will benefit from doing them occasionally. Try to ask leading questions such as "Do

TIP: Early in your new position find out what your district uses as a performance evaluation document to get an indication of how the district perceives your job.

you expect the library to be open after hours?" or state "I would like to initiate flexible scheduling and here's why." Always be prepared to back up anything you initiate.

Your performance evaluation document can communicate all the things that you do. If your district does not have a separate instrument for librarians, get a good one for your principal to look at. It delineates your responsibilities so well that your principal knows exactly what your job is and can discuss your needs with more insight. A well-informed principal can help you get time with the teachers for curriculum planning and promote you to the teachers; she can give you the kind of budget support you need for print and online resources, and she can support your scheduling needs by not assigning you unreasonable duties.

3 ORDERING AND PROCESSING MATERIALS

This chapter includes the technical aspects of selecting, ordering, preparing, and using books, periodicals, audiovisual materials, and equipment. The appendices include lists of book vendors, sources of current book reviews, and sources for retrospective book reviews. You will also find lists of supplies appropriate to each media area as well as sources for general library supplies.

BOOK SELECTION

Book selection is an ongoing process. No matter when you order books, you will find yourself doing something related to book selection every day of the year. As you use and learn the collection, you will find weak areas that need special purchases to bring those sections up to date. Your knowledge of the collection will give you a special perspective as you use other selection procedures.

Get recommendations and lists of requested materials from teachers and administrators. Buy them if at all possible. You will then be prepared when a teacher makes an assignment of a particular book. Ask librarians from other schools with similar curriculum. Frequently, shared information about the same curriculum can result in finding excellent materials to fill in gaps in a collection.

Bibliographies from textbooks and other materials used in the curriculum are a source, but they should be used with caution as many might be out of date or simply unavailable. Consider any recommended readings or supplemental material used in class.

Use selection aids review material so you can get some background on particular items. Different reviewers judge things differently. If possible, look at more than one review. Some online sites and databases will have reviews from different sources. Even commercial sites such as amazon.com and barnesandnoble.com have reviews from a variety of sources, including their customers.

Find out what students are interested in reading. Establish a student committee to make recommendations or do a reader interest survey.

Meeting the curriculum needs is your ultimate goal. All these

---

How are books selected?
- consultation with teachers
- textbook bibliographies
- selection aids
- consultation with students
- consideration files

TIP: Spend your money early in the year, so if an order is not completely filled, you will have time to spend that money. Hold only a small portion of your budget for late-in-the-year requests from teachers.

sources help you create a consideration file and compile suggestions. An easy way to keep track of potential purchases is to use note cards in your consideration file to record both individual entries and general subjects to look for in the selection tools. Or you might find it easier to begin a list in a word-processing program or spreadsheet, adding titles as you go and then saving it.

Do a subject search in an electronic database, print off that page with the bibliographic information, and put that into the consideration file. Assign a priority number to each entry and group priorities together or maintain a different electronic list for each priority. Make photocopies of reviews and keep a hard copy in your consideration file. When you get ready to place an order, you will have pertinent information in one place, a great help in deciding whether to change a title from one priority to another.

SELECTION TOOLS

There are many selection tools available to help you choose books and other materials. Appendices E and F list a variety of resources that are widely used by school library media specialists.

You will want to subscribe to at least one professional journal that includes current reviews. Each month when it arrives, read reviews of materials. If you generate your book orders electronically, you might find that it is most convenient to add an item to your order, save it, and print or submit the order later.

The most commonly subscribed to journals for school librarians are *School Library Journal* and *Booklist*; however, there are several others you should review on a regular basis and subscribe to if money allows. These journals deal only with newly published materials. If you want retrospective reviews of older materials, check sources such as *Elementary, Junior High*, or *Senior High School Catalogs* (published by H. W. Wilson).

PERIODICAL AND ONLINE SERVICES SELECTION

Periodical selection is not as complex as book selection and has changed drastically since online databases have become so easily accessible. While print indexes have become obsolete and many libraries have abandoned their rows and rows of thick books, because of technology the face of print periodical acquisition is different.

All those vital back issues of current news magazines are rapidly becoming a thing of the past because that same material is available through online subscription databases. So the role of print periodicals now becomes up-to-date curriculum support and pleasure reading. Studies have shown that young adults have so little time for pleasure reading that for many of them browsing magazines is the extent of their reading for recreation. Some popular periodicals can continue to be the draw that brings students into the library.

With a subscription to an online service, you might have to spend a larger portion of your budget on this format and will need to cut back on your print periodicals. Teacher and student input is more valuable than ever. Keep a count of the periodicals that are left laying on the tables during a given time to get a record of which magazines are read.

Subscriptions to online databases are expensive, but if all the schools in your district select the same service, you can get a price reduction. If yours is a small district and there is no district coordinator to negotiate with online vendors for you, get together and do the negotiating yourself. Everyone can benefit from the cooperation.

Another option for you to consider is membership in a consortium or network. There could be a financial cost involved or you might have to agree to making your collection available for interlibrary loan. In return, you will be able to participate in an online database subscription that would otherwise be too expensive for you. This can dramatically increase the amount of periodical material you have.

Given the unlimited array of resources on the Internet, is it actually possible to "select" online resources? Yes it is, to some extent. You decide whether to subscribe to certain databases, both fee-based and free. You decide on Web sites to recommend to parents, students, and teachers. You have access to government information. Eventually, you will want to include lessons on the skills needed by students to evaluate the information they find on the Internet. So the Internet requires just as much of your skill in selection as any other information resource.

One reason filtering advocates give for having filtering software is that there is a selection process the material goes through before the student receives it. However, this selection process deals only with words or Web sites, not the kind of thoughtful consideration you give to selecting information sources. If you find a useful health or other site that is blocked by your filtering software, find out the process for unblocking that site so you and your students can have the benefit of that material.

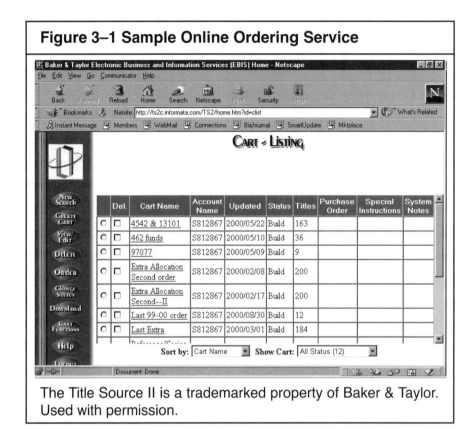

Figure 3–1 Sample Online Ordering Service

The Title Source II is a trademarked property of Baker & Taylor. Used with permission.

ORDERING MATERIALS

The easiest way is to order everything through one vendor so you have one payment and one invoice.

If you order all your materials from one vendor, you can usually get a better discount. Your district might already be committed to a certain vendor. If not, you can get an additional discount by entering into an informal agreement with other librarians to use the same vendor. Compare vendors' prices and services. Most provide clerical services such as lists, ease of ordering, and MARC records for your circulation system. It is advisable to order one and a half to two times the amount budgeted. One way to handle this is to send a vendor three priority lists. You want everything you can get on list one; you then want as much as you can get on list two; then, if there is any money left over, you want as much as you can get from list three. (See Appendix A for book vendors and their addresses.)

Electronic ordering has simplified this process (see Figure 3–1). You can now access inventories and estimate fill rates based on the online availability of information. You can tell instantly if a

Figure 3–2 EBSCO Sample Renewal List

EBSCO
SUBSCRIPTION SERVICES

P.O. BOX 2543
BIRMINGHAM, AL 35202 / 205/ 991-1211 / TELEX 78-2663

EBSCO
Industries,
Inc.

ANNUAL RENEWAL LIST

EBSCO CUSTOMER NAME
CUSTOMER ADDRESS
CITY, STATE   ZIP

		PAGE NO
RENEWAL LIST NO.	16	1
AA	ACCT. NO.	BR-00000-00
	DATE	JUNE 1, 1990

TITLE CODE	QTY. (IF MORE THAN 1)	NAME OF PUBLICATION	FOR	STARTING	★ PRICE UNIT	EXTENSION
		THIS RENEWAL LIST INCLUDES ALL SUBSCRIPTION ORDERS INVOICED THROUGH 04/20/90. IF A RECENT CHANGE IN YOUR RENEWAL LIST, SUCH AS CANCELLATION OR ADDITION DOES NOT APPEAR, THEY MISSED THE RENEWAL LIST PRODUCTION CUT-OFF DATE INDICATED ABOVE. THESE CHANGES ARE RECORDED IN OUR FILE AND WILL BE AUTOMATICALLY INCORPORATED INTO YOUR RENEWAL INVOICE.				
		SEND TO— 10 EBSCO CUSTOMER NAME CUSTOMER ADDRESS CITY, STATE ZIP	TERM SHOWN BELOW WILL BE ORDERED NONCANCELLABLE APPLIES AFTER RENEWAL ORDER IS PROCESSED.			
041 872 003	1	AMERICAN HISTORY ILLUSTRATED **L1** *BM** 0089831 (SP)	1 YR	09-01-90	20 00	20 00
227 676 145	1	COMPUTE! MAGAZINE/**/CDS/ **L1** **MO** 0085358 (SP)	1 YR	09-01-90	19 94	19 94

245 008 008	1	CRICKET/THE MAGAZINE FOR
		      CHILDREN/ /**/ /NEO/
		L1 **MO**
		      0085358 (SP)
		NO ODD TERMS (C)
			1 YR	09-01-90	24 97	24 97

277 335 162	1	DISCOVER/THE NEWS MAGAZINE OF
		      SCIENCE/**/
		L1 **MO**
		      0085358 (SP)
			1 YR	09-01-90	27 00	27 00

612 117 002	1	NATIONAL GEOGRAPHIC/INCL/FREE
		      INDEX/SURFACE MAIL/
		      /ALL EXCEPT CANADA/
		L1 **MO**
		      0089831 (SP)
			1 YR	09-01-90	22 50	22 50

801 459 009	1	SCHOOL LIBRARY JOURNAL **L1** **MO** 0089831 (SP)	1 YR	09-01-90	63 00	63 00

892 081 001	1	TIME/DOMESTIC ED/ /AWUA9//**/
		/FOR US & POSSESSIONS ONLY/
		/SURFACE MAIL/
		                                     WK
		      0089831 (SP)
			1 YR	09-01-90	58 24	58 24

		CONTINUED ON NEXT PAGE				

ABBREVIATION KEY ON REVERSE SIDE

EBS380 (Printed in USA)

NOTE: PRICES SHOWN ARE CURRENTLY KNOWN PUBLISHERS PRICES, AND ARE
       SUBJECT TO CHANGE UNTIL THE PUBLISHERS ACCEPT THE RENEWAL ORDERS.

title is still in print or out of stock. Leave off any titles that are not available and improve your fill rate. Some vendors include reviews in their ordering system so you can use the system itself as a selection tool.

If there are important reference books that you order every year, arrange a standing order for these materials. You will receive an update for the book you request as soon as it is published. Because you request the book before it is published, you could qualify for a discount. H. W. Wilson and Gale are two publishers that have standing order programs for materials frequently used by school media centers.

WHAT ABOUT ORDERING MAGAZINES?

If you order all your periodicals from one vendor, it will simplify your clerical and bookkeeping task. When it is time to reorder, the vendor will send a listing of current subscriptions for your review to delete or add (see Figure 3–2). Periodical vendors are listed in Appendix B.

HOW ARE NEWSPAPERS ORDERED?

You will probably order newspapers directly from the publisher, although a few national papers might be available from your serials vendor. When ordering, check for special rates for schools; there might be a reduced rate for the school year. Choose the best of local, state, and national newspapers to represent a variety of interests and viewpoints. Decide if you need those national papers in print since they are probably available online.

HOW IS A BOOK ORDER REQUISITION FILLED OUT?

The easiest way is to write a "Do Not Exceed" note on the requisition and supply a list of titles (see Figure 3–3). The vendor already knows your specifications for processing and you will already have negotiated any additional cost per book. It is not necessary to state individual book prices on your purchase order.

Many vendors have methods of verifying and ordering books electronically. CD-ROMs and Web sites help you put a book order together. You might have to print off this list and submit it to your purchasing department to get approval for your order. Or you might be able to do your book order automatically with your circulation system.

HOW DOES THE VENDOR KNOW WHAT TYPE OF PROCESSING TO INCLUDE?

The first time you order from a vendor, you fill out a form with all of your cataloging specifications (see Figure 3–4). "Fully pro-

TIP: Information on the online ordering system lets you know if a title is not available so you can leave it off your order and improve your fill rate.

Figure 3–3 "Do Not Exceed" Instructions

<table>
<tr>
<td colspan="4" align="center">**REQUISITION FORM**</td>
</tr>
<tr>
<td colspan="4" align="center">DATE ORIGINATED</td>
</tr>
<tr>
<td colspan="2">To: **PURCHASING DEPARTMENT**
NAME OF DEPARTMENT PROCESSING REQUISITION
PURCHASING, ETC.</td>
<td colspan="2">REQUIRED FOR:
Lincoln High School
(AD. BLDG., SCHOOL, ETC.)</td>
</tr>
<tr>
<td colspan="2">DEPARTMENT:
Media Center
(MATH, SCI., PLUMBING, ETC.)</td>
<td colspan="2">SHIP TO:

(IF DIFFERENT THAN ABOVE)</td>
</tr>
<tr>
<td colspan="2">BUDGET LINE
ITEM NUMBER</td>
<td>ORIGINATOR/RECIPIENT</td>
<td>Date
Required</td>
</tr>
<tr>
<td>QUANTITY</td>
<td>SIZE</td>
<td>DESCRIPTION - TELL HERE WHAT IS WANTED
EXPLAIN FULLY - SHOW SUGGESTED SOURCES</td>
<td>PRICE EACH | PRICE TOTAL</td>
</tr>
<tr><td></td><td></td><td>PLEASE ORDER THE ATTACHED LIST</td><td></td></tr>
<tr><td></td><td></td><td>OF BOOKS FROM:</td><td></td></tr>
<tr><td></td><td></td><td>Baker & Taylor</td><td></td></tr>
<tr><td></td><td></td><td>380 Edison Way</td><td></td></tr>
<tr><td></td><td></td><td>Reno, NV 89564</td><td></td></tr>
<tr><td></td><td></td><td></td><td></td></tr>
<tr><td></td><td></td><td></td><td></td></tr>
<tr><td></td><td></td><td></td><td></td></tr>
<tr><td></td><td></td><td></td><td></td></tr>
<tr><td></td><td></td><td></td><td></td></tr>
<tr><td></td><td></td><td></td><td></td></tr>
<tr><td></td><td></td><td>Do not exceed $3,000.00</td><td></td></tr>
<tr><td></td><td></td><td>see attached list for titles</td><td></td></tr>
<tr><td></td><td></td><td></td><td></td></tr>
<tr><td></td><td></td><td></td><td></td></tr>
<tr><td></td><td></td><td></td><td></td></tr>
<tr>
<td colspan="3">APPROVAL SIGNATURES - REQUIRED WHEN TOTAL EXCEEDS THE AMOUNT SHOWN BY TITLE</td>
<td>TOTAL
OF THIS
REQUISITION</td>
</tr>
<tr>
<td colspan="3">PRINCIPAL   DATE</td>
<td></td>
</tr>
<tr>
<td colspan="3">SUPERINTENDENT   DATE</td>
<td></td>
</tr>
</table>

Figure 3–4 Cataloging Specifications Form

Cataloging Specifications for **ABRIDGED DEWEY**

(Please, only complete this specification form, or the one on the following page, if you require hardcopy or electronic cataloging.)

LETTER CAPITALIZATION			* ☐ **All CAPS** ☐ Upper & lower case
SUBJECT HEADINGS			* ☐ **Sears** ☐ Library of Congress ☐ None ☐ LC Children's Defaults to LC when children's headings are not available and suppresses Juvenile in the LC heading.
PROCESSING KITS			* ☐ One per book ☐ One per title
MAIN ENTRY CARDS		301	☐ Not required * ☐ **2 provided with each card set** ☐ ___ Number of additional cards

FICTION	Classification	102	* ☐ **F**	☐ FIC	☐ Fiction	☐ None
	Author/Main Entry Letters	110	☐ 1 ☐ Up to 7	☐ 2 ☐ ALL	* ☐ **3** ☐ Other ___	☐ None
NONFICTION	Classification	100	* ☐ **Abridged Dewey Number**		☐ None	
	Classification Number Length	137	Not applicable for this option.			
	Author/Main Entry Letters	115	☐ 1 ☐ Up to 7	☐ 2 ☐ ALL	* ☐ **3** ☐ Other ___	☐ None
EASY FICTION	Classification	105	☐ Same as your choice for fiction ☐ F ☐ Fiction ☐ FIC ☐ None		* ☐ **E**	
	Author/Main Entry Letters	113	☐ Same as your choice for fiction ☐ 1 ☐ Up to 7	☐ 2 ☐ ALL	☐ 3 ☐ Other ___	* ☐ **None**
EASY NONFICTION	Classification	106	☐ Same as your choice for nonfiction * ☐ **E** ☐ None			
	Author/Main Entry Letters	118	* ☐ **Same as your choice for nonfiction** ☐ 1 ☐ Up to 7	☐ 2 ☐ ALL	☐ 3 ☐ Other ___	* ☐ **None**
STORY COLLECTION	Classification	143	* ☐ **Same as your choice for fiction** ☐ 808.8 ☐ SC ☐ 808.83 ☐ SS ☐ Dewey # as assigned by LC	☐ None		
	Author/Main Entry Letters		☐ 1 ☐ Up to 7	☐ 2 ☐ ALL	☐ 3 ☐ Other ___	☐ None
INDIVIDUAL BIOGRAPHY	Classification	103	* ☐ **B**	☐ 92	☐ 921	☐ None
	Biographee's Letters	120	* ☐ **Complete Surname** ☐ 1 ☐ Up to 7	☐ 2 ☐ Other ___	☐ 3	☐ None
	Author Letters	123	* ☐ **None** ☐ Up to 7	☐ 1 ☐ ALL	☐ 2 ☐ Other ___	☐ 3
COLLECTIVE BIOGRAPHY	Classification	104	☐ 92	* ☐ **920**	☐ None	
	Author Letters	126	☐ 1 ☐ Up to 7	☐ 2 ☐ ALL	* ☐ **3** ☐ Other ___	☐ None
PREFIXES	Reference	143	* ☐ **No prefix provided**		☐ R	☐ REF
	Juvenile	141	* ☐ **No prefix provided**		☐ J	☐ JUV
	Customized		Contact Customer Service for details.			

*Denotes Internal Use only

cessed" books have a computer record that conforms to MARC specifications, a bar code wherever you choose, an affixed spine label, a plastic cover on the dust jacket, and a card and a pocket on the inside. Unless you have ample clerical help, it is advisable to order shelf-ready materials to free your time for more professional activities. You will receive a disk containing cataloging information that you can upload into your system or network.

Whatever specifications you give to a vendor with your order are kept on file. It is best to use the same format every time you place an order unless you have a very good reason to change. This will assure consistency.

WHAT TYPE OF BINDING SHOULD YOU REQUEST?

In many cases library binding is the best binding for items you know will be heavily circulated. However, if you need an item that you know will not get a lot of use, you could use trade binding and save some money. Plastic-bound paperbacks can help you get more mileage out of the eye-catching paperbacks that are popular. If you want titles that are faddish and will be discarded once the fad is over or can be easily disposed of when they get worn out, paperbacks are a reasonable choice.

> **Types of binding**
> - library binding
> - trade
> - paperback
> - plastic-bound paperback

> **TIP:** If your automated system does not allow you access to collection statistics until the end of the year, keep an informal tally of additions and withdrawals so you will know your collection size at any time.

PROCESSING MATERIALS

WHAT TO DO WHEN BOOKS ARRIVE FROM THE VENDOR

Write down a standard set of procedures so processing will be done the same way no matter who does the physical labor when books arrive. A common set of procedures includes the following steps:

1. Make sure the invoice number matches the number on the packing slip, box label, or any paperwork that comes with the order. Do not start any processing until you have an invoice.
2. Find your original order and check books against the order.
3. Check books against the packing slip.
4. Place books in a designated place if cataloging is needed.
5. Record date and initial the purchase order.
6. Record amount of the order on the budget control form.
7. Note on your original order and consideration file any books that are out of print (O.P.) and no longer available,

as well as those that are temporarily out of stock (T.O.S) and can be ordered later.

8. Send purchase order and invoice to the appropriate person for payment.

If you are part of a district that has centralized processing, you might not have to do these steps, but it is valuable to know the process.

GETTING BOOKS READY TO CHECK OUT

Before processing, check the physical condition of the books. If you are not satisfied with any book, you can return it *before* you have placed any property marks on it. Check the call number and the computer record. You do not have to use the cataloging provided, either, if you do not agree with it because of existing cataloging in the library or your own expertise. Use the following procedures to get a book ready to check out:

1. Look in the catalog to see if the book is a duplicate. If you already have a copy, make sure the call number is the same. Then download the disk and place the bar code on the book, if not already attached. On the part of the computer record where copy information is recorded, add the price and any other copy-specific information you wish to keep.
2. If the book is a duplicate, decide if you want to change or add anything to the call number. This change must be made on the record and on the book. Some additions could be "Reference" or "c. 2."
3. Decide if you want to keep all of the subject headings and added entries provided in your record.
4. Stamp your school name on the book.
5. If you still maintain a card shelflist, note price on shelflist card. In addition, add the date and vendor name.
6. Add a security device to the book according to manufacturer's instructions.
7. Attach a book pocket and cover the dust jacket with a plastic cover, if necessary.
8. Finally, add the title to any appropriate bibliographies. You might wish to keep an informal count so you will know how many books and which categories have been added to your collection. Your circulation system might be able to report these at any time, making a handwritten system unnecessary.

TIP: As soon as books are ready to check out, find the items that were recommended by faculty members. Drop them a note telling them their request has come in and it is ready for use.

Figure 3–5 Periodical Check-In Form (Spreadsheet)												
2000–01 Periodicals												
Title	Jan.	Feb.	March	April	May	June	July	August	Sept.	Oct.	Nov.	Dec.
Booklist	X											
Biography												
Discovery	X											
Highlights for Children												
National Geographic	X											
School Library Journal	X											

WHAT IF THE BOOKS DO NOT COME WITH COMPUTER RECORDS?

Cataloging and classification information is readily accessible now with the Library of Congress catalog available online *www.loc.gov/marc/marcservice.html*). Here you will find instructions on using the system. Once you locate the record you need, you can enter the date in the template in your automated system. Web sites that allow you to actually download MARC records for a fee are listed at the Library of Congress Web site. You can then edit the records to fit your system requirements and your existing collection practices. In addition to saving time, commercial cataloging will be consistent with standardized procedures. You will want to maintain the integrity of your catalog by keeping your records clean and consistent.

WHAT TO DO WHEN PERIODICALS ARRIVE?

As with books, write down a standard set of procedures for processing. Here are procedures you might want to use:

1. Using the invoice, make out an inventory card for each magazine ordered, design a check-in sheet to put on a clipboard or in a notebook, or use a spreadsheet (see Figure 3–5). If volunteers or aides are helping you check in magazines, a handwritten system works well. If one person is checking them in, a spreadsheet will do well.
2. File cards or sheets in alphabetical order.
3. As each periodical arrives, note whether the magazine will

TIP: Save wear and tear on magazines by buying plastic covers. Covers also make the magazine secure. They are available from library supply companies.

TIP: Magazines that are to be thrown away can be cut up for vertical file materials or art projects.

be routed or if there are articles to copy and share with the staff.

4. Check the issue on the card.
5. Stamp your school name on the cover and on selected pages throughout. Be sure to find blank spaces for the stamp.
6. Prepare magazines for the shelf.
7. If magazines are to be checked out, you might want to put blank book cards and pockets on as you process them. Cards should be placed inside the front or back cover. Put the name and the date of the magazine on each card. This could be the only item you check out by a handwritten method. You might be able to check them out using your circulation system by making one record per magazine and keeping the bar codes in a Rolodex.
8. Put magazines on the shelf.

HOW ARE MAGAZINES ARRANGED ON THE SHELF?

The most common arrangement is to place magazines in alphabetical order by title. However, you could choose to arrange them by subject. Subject arrangement is helpful when the periodical collection is large.

Decide how many current issues are to be kept on the shelf. As new issues of magazines are put out, the old issues should be moved to your storage area or discarded.

Decide how long to keep old magazines in your storage area. Depending on available space, magazines are usually kept three to ten years. With the rise of online databases, back files are not as critical to research. Magazines can be stored in files available from library supply companies. The best arrangement for files is alphabetical order by title, with individual issues arranged by cover date.

AUDIOVISUAL MATERIALS

Selection of audiovisual materials must be done carefully because the cost of those materials means that you will be quite limited in the number of items you can purchase. Since each item must be exactly what your school needs, preview of audiovisual materials becomes as valuable to you as reviews from outside sources. Use the Nonprint Evaluation Form (see Figure 3–6) to evaluate the appropriateness of specific materials for your library's collection.

Work with teachers so you know where the weak areas in your

Figure 3–6 Nonprint Evaluation Form

Title _____

Subject of Curriculum Use _____

Producer _____ Date _____ Price _____ Distributor _____

Grade Level _____ Reading Level _____ Classification _____

Recommend for Purchase: Yes_____ No _____ Priority: _____ Essential _____

Marginal_____

Specify Media: _____ Cassette _____ Laser Disk

_____ CD-ROM _____ Recording

_____ Computer Program _____ Slides: _____ b&w _____ color

_____ Kit _____ Other _____

Specify the purpose or curriculum tie-in for which the medium could be used

_____

Use the appropriate key to indicate your rating in accordance with the audience and objective that was specified. Key: P = Poor F = Fair G = Good E = Excellent NA = Not applicable

	Key:	Comments:
1. Relevancy to the curriculum	_____	_____
2. Accuracy and authenticity	_____	_____
3. Organization of content	_____	_____
4. Scope (suitable number of concepts)	_____	_____
5. Suitability of length	_____	_____
6. Stimulation of student interest for further discussion or study	_____	_____
7. Technical aspects	_____	_____
8. Evaluation of accompanying materials (teachers' guide, notes, etc.)	_____	_____

Summary:

_____
_____
_____

Evaluation:

_____
_____
_____
_____

Reviewed Source (s): _____ Date _____

Evaluator (s) _____ School _____ Date _____

TIP: If you are able to preview an audiovisual item before purchasing, invite teachers to preview it with you so you can get their input.

audiovisual collection are. Get recommendations and lists of requested items for materials from teachers and administrators, and buy those items if at all possible. Consider any items recommended or listed in bibliographies from textbooks and other materials used in the curriculum.

Many selection aids review audiovisual materials. Different reviewers rate items differently, so if possible, look at more than one review. Create a consideration file, making a note of where each item was reviewed. As with books, you can make photocopies of reviews to put in your consideration file.

Of course, consider your collection. For example, do you need some audiovisual materials on a particular subject?

What selection tools are most useful when selecting audiovisual materials? Most library media specialists subscribe to at least the following sources: *Booklist, School Library Journal,* and *Media & Methods,* which are review sources for media. An expanded list is in Appendix F.

TIP: Before ordering audiovisual materials, be sure they are compatible with the equipment you have.

HOW ARE AUDIOVISUAL MATERIALS ORDERED?

Go through an audiovisual representative who represents several audiovisual companies or order directly from individual companies. Some book wholesalers now carry audiovisual titles and can offer cataloging and discounts.

Special discounts or bonuses are offered when you buy in volume. If your order is not large enough to qualify for a special price, get together with other schools and make one large order.

More and more, audiovisual companies are offering cataloging and will send you a disk with the records.

WHAT TO DO WHEN AUDIOVISUAL MATERIALS ARRIVE

As with books and magazines, write down a standard set of procedures for processing. Here are some recommended procedures:

1. Make sure there is an invoice in the box. Do not start any processing until you have an invoice.
2. Find your original order. Check audiovisual titles against the school purchase order and the packing slip.
3. Make sure the item works as it should before you go any farther with your processing. If it does not work, you can send it back. If you have your property stamp anywhere on the item, you can not return it.
4. Record the invoice price on the record. Place audiovisual materials in a designated place if they need cataloging.
5. Record the date of receipt and initial the purchase order. Record the amount of the order in your budget. Note on

your original order and consideration file any audiovisual titles that are no longer available and those that are temporarily out of stock and can be ordered later. Send the purchase order and invoice to the appropriate person for payment.

GETTING AUDIOVISUAL MATERIALS READY TO CHECK OUT

If you have not done so, make sure you are satisfied with the operation of the material. Check the cataloging if that has been provided with the material. Remember, you can edit any cataloging provided by the vendor if you do not agree with it.

The following procedures will help you prepare the materials for library use:

1. As with books, look in the catalog to see whether the item is a duplicate. If you already have a copy, decide if you want both copies in the same place. Occasionally, you will want the same item in two places if teachers frequently look for an item in an alternative location, e.g., history teachers might look in the 900s for an item about a battle that is usually in the 300s.
2. If the item is a duplicate, you might want to change the call number on the old item as well. Be sure to change the call number on the record as well as the item. If the item is not a duplicate, decide if you want to change or add anything to the call number. Again, make those changes on both the record and the item. Decide if you want to keep all of the subject headings and added entries.
3. Stamp your school name on the item.
4. On items such as CDs or audiocassettes, you can write the school name on them with a permanent fine-tip marker.
5. In order to have a current count of the size of your collection, keep a record of additions and withdrawals according to call numbers if your circulation system does not figure these until the end of the year.
6. Add a security device to the item, if possible, and attach a book pocket. If your library is computerized, data must be entered into the computer by hand or downloaded from a disk provided by the vendor. Then a bar code must be placed on the item. Add the title to any appropriate bibliographies.

SELECTING AUDIOVISUAL EQUIPMENT

As technology becomes a larger part of the school environment, you might find that you are part of a team in the purchase of

TIP: Promote your new materials by keeping a list of them at the main circulation desk. Your automated system can print out a list of these titles for you and you can keep it in an eye-catching list or folder.

audiovisual equipment in packages. You are in a unique position for this purchase decision because you have access to the equipment and can see how it operates, you see how teachers use that equipment, and frequently vendors and information come to you first.

To prepare for this, be aware of the equipment as teachers ask for it. Do teachers need classroom-size boom boxes with detachable speakers or do they need more portable players? Do you need televisions or monitors to go with videocassette recorders or with computers? When you determine your equipment needs, you can develop specifications based on those needs before you buy. You might be bound to the school's guidelines and procedures for acquiring the actual equipment.

Read current literature in professional journals on trends and developments in the manufacture of audiovisual equipment. Watch for innovations in equipment.

When you know what you want the equipment to do, you can apply these more general criteria:

1. Portability: Is the equipment compact and lightweight? Does it need to be?
2. Sturdiness: Is the equipment strong enough for everyday use?
3. Ease of operation: Does the operation make sense even for inexperienced operators?
4. Performance standards: Does the equipment work dependably?
5. Is it easy to maintain and repair?
6. Are service and support from the manufacturer or distributor available? Can you get bulbs and supplies?
7. What is its cost effectiveness?

Sources of equipment information are found in Appendix D.

HOW IS AUDIOVISUAL EQUIPMENT ORDERED?

Know school and district policies. When ordering more than one piece of equipment, you might qualify for discounts. If there is no district coordinator for media centers, you could coordinate with other librarians to order the same items at the same time from the same source in order to negotiate for a discount. Determine whether or not you need bids. Your school or district policy will state the dollar amount that requires you to obtain a bid.

If you need bids, assemble specifications for all equipment to be ordered. Be sure the specifications are well written to eliminate poor quality or off-brand items that will not meet your needs.

Key selection factors
- needs
- school guidelines
- trends

TIP: The lowest bid is not always the best bid. You might need to honor the bid of a local supplier who is a taxpayer of your district and contributes to the school in other ways.

3–7 Inventory Maintenance Card and Checklist					
Inventory No./ Serial No.	Equipment Type & Model	Date of Purchase	Battery/ Lamp	Inventory Date and Condition(poor, fair, good)	Repair Record date/work done

Send a copy of the specs to all interested suppliers. Select the best bid.

WHAT TO DO WHEN THE EQUIPMENT ARRIVES

Here is a procedure you can use to prepare audiovisual equipment for school use:

1. Check invoice and purchase order against the packing slip.
2. Write the date of receipt on the purchase order.
3. Make sure the equipment is what you ordered.
4. Make sure the equipment is in good working order.
5. Record the invoice amount on your budget.
6. Tag equipment as school property in a permanent manner with an engraving pen or paint pen.
7. Make a Rolodex card with the bar code for checking out purposes.
8. Make a computer record or card (see Figure 3–7) for your circulation system and all pertinent information for maintenance and inventory purposes.
9. Send the purchase order and invoice to the appropriate person for payment.
10. If necessary for insurance, send equipment information, such as serial and model numbers, to the appropriate office.
11. Prepare equipment for checkout.

12. Stamp your school name on the operator's manual.
13. Keep all equipment manuals in a secure file.
14. Make sure you have the supplies you need to operate the equipment, e.g., power cords, remotes, tapes, bulbs, and so on.

4 CATALOGING

If a book is not already cataloged and processed when it arrives at your library's door, how do you prepare it for use? A checklist form can provide a list of things to do to each individual book and help you develop a written set of procedures so the labor can be shared easily with clerical help or volunteers or a centralized processing department. Here is a basic list of things to do to process a book if it needs original cataloging:

- Look in the catalog to see if the title is a duplicate. If it is, use the procedures for a processed book outlined in Chapter 3 (see "Getting Books Ready to Check Out").
- Assign a call number and compare with other books in your collection.
- Assign subject headings. Make sure they are as accurate as possible. Compare with other subjects in the catalog or in your authority file.
- Proceed with the steps outlined for cataloging, classifying, and processing books (see Figure 4–1).

Many catalogs, including the Library of Congress, are available online if you wish to look at someone else's cataloging of the item you have. You can get some ideas for call numbers, subject headings, and other parts of the record. You could join a consortium of libraries that will allow you to download the computer record that you find. However, it is still imperative that you edit the record for your users.

NOTE: The Dewey Decimal Classification system is the preferred system of classification in most school libraries. Some high schools use the Library of Congress classification system, but in this book the focus will be on Dewey.

CLASSIFICATION

HOW IS A CALL NUMBER ASSIGNED TO A BOOK?

Although there are shortcuts, a basic understanding of the Dewey Decimal Classification system is needed. The Dewey system divides all knowledge into ten categories:

000–009	General works
100–199	Philosophy
200–299	Religion
300–399	Social sciences
400–499	Language
500–599	Pure science

Figure 4–1 Checklist for Cataloging, Classifying, and Processing Books

THIS BOOK NEEDS:
CATALOGING
CLASSIFYING
PROCESSING _____CHECK HERE
    IF BOOK IS
    NEW—ALL
    PROCESSING

CHECK BELOW IF BOOK
NEEDS THESE ITEMS ONLY
1. MARKS OF OWNERSHIP
    CAREER STICKER
    REFERENCE STICKER OR STAMP
    OTHER
2. SPINE LABELS
    "CAREER" LABEL
    "REFERENCE" LABEL
    OTHER
3. POCKET
    JACKET
    MENDING
    DISCARDING
4. BARCODE
5. NOTIFY_____
6. OTHER
PROBLEM?
WHAT:

600–699	Applied science (technology)
700–799	Fine arts
800–899	Literature
900–999	General geography and history

Each general category or class is subdivided into ten subclasses, such as

900	History-travel
910	Geography
920	Biography
930	Ancient History

940	Europe
950	Asia
960	Africa
970	North America
980	South America
990	Pacific Islands

Each of the subclasses can be divided into ten sections:

970	North America
971	Canada
972	Mexico
973	United States
974	Northeastern States
975	Southeastern States
976	Southcentral States
977	Northcentral States
978	Western States
979	Far Western States

As each subject narrows, the category is divided using decimal points:

975	Southeastern states
975.1	Delaware
975.2	Maryland
975.3	District of Columbia
975.4	West Virginia
975.5	Virginia
975.6	North Carolina
975.7	South Carolina
975.8	Georgia
975.9	Florida

Some books have different identifications that are not part of the Dewey classification scheme. For example:

F or Fic	fiction books
SC or SS	a story collection or short story collection, but these usually are treated as fiction
E	"easy" materials or for materials designed for children in primary grades; some schools use other symbols or designations for "easy" materials
R or Ref	"Reference" material that does not circulate; used above a classification number.
B	individual biography; 92 or 921 can also be used

Additional symbols are added to a call number for any kind of special collection, such as "C" for "Careers."

Under the classification part of the call number, the first letter of the author's last name usually is used. Some school media specialists use the first two or three letters of the author's last name. Use whatever system you prefer or what has been used previously in your library. Examples:

F	F	R	Ref
S	SAN	427	427
		W	WEB

For individual biographies, the subject's last name is used in the call number instead of the author's name. For example, a biography of Longfellow might be labeled:

B	(or)	92	(or)	921
Lon		Lo		L

Dewey number assignments can be found in other places besides the records you do yourself. Cataloging information often appears in recently published books; on the verso (reverse side) of the title page is sample cataloging with complete bibliographic data.

Reviews in selection tools such as the *Elementary School Catalog*, *Junior High School Catalog*, *High School Catalog*, *Booklist*, and *School Library Journal* frequently include Dewey classification numbers and subject headings. Make notes in your consideration file of the suggested call numbers and subject headings.

Because of the ease of computerized cataloging, you might be tempted to weed your print copies of *Sears List of Subject Headings* or *Library of Congress Subject Headings* and your *Dewey Decimal Classification*. However, when you are faced with doing your own cataloging, these volumes provide invaluable information that will help you do an intimidating task. If your's is a new library and these tools were not purchased, check with the librarians at older schools.

HOW IS A SUBJECT HEADING ASSIGNED TO A BOOK?

Assign a subject heading that describes as closely as possible the entire book. Standard subject headings can be found in several places, beginning with your own catalog. If subject headings that are provided do not match what is in your catalog, check in the latest edition of the *Sears List of Subject Headings* or use the *Library of Congress Subject Headings*. Review sources also make subject heading suggestions. If you make notes in your consider-

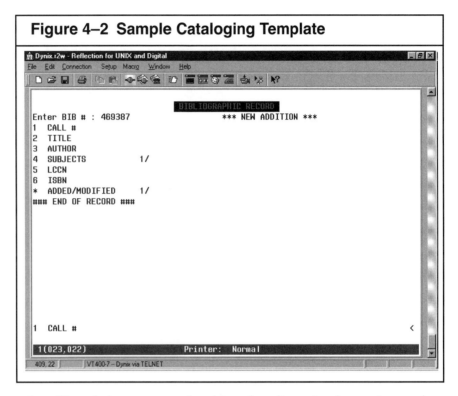

Figure 4–2 Sample Cataloging Template

ation file of the suggested subject headings in the reviews, they will be easy to find when you need them. Most electronic catalogs have an authority file to record all subject headings used in your catalog. This will keep your subject headings consistent. If you use a subject heading that is not in the authority file, simply add it. You might wish to add subjects that are in the language your students would be more likely to use. Add these to your authority file if you think you will need access to them later.

You might need more than one subject heading to describe the whole book. Too many subject headings, however, can waste your time and frustrate your students if subjects are very similar. You need just enough subject headings to describe a book fully so your students can find the various kinds of information it contains. However, your automated catalog might be able to accommodate more subject headings to benefit your students.

HOW TO CATALOG A BOOK

Cataloging books is the process of creating a record that will go into the computer catalog and serve as an index to help students find the books they need.

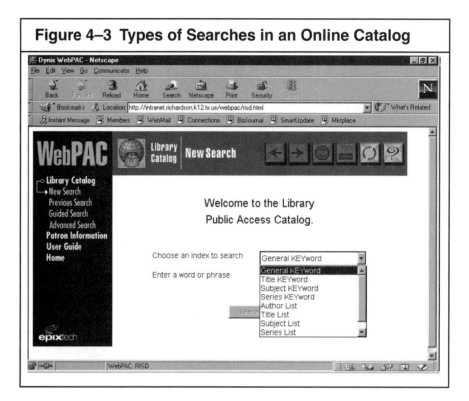

Figure 4–3 Types of Searches in an Online Catalog

With a basic understanding of cataloging principles, you can handle the cataloging challenges you will face. Essentially, you will have a blank template with basic information that you need to fill in (see Figure 4–2). A record will include:

- *Author*: Author's last name first, if there is an author.
- *Title*: Whether you include the beginning "A," "An," or "The" or not, make sure the codes are correct so the title will be traced by the first important word.
- *Physical description*: This must include number of pages. Include illustrations, if any.
- *Publisher*: Name of publisher is required and date of publication. If you have a place of publication, put it before the publisher.
- *Subject(s)*: You might be limited by your system. Use the most descriptive subjects according to your need.
- *Added fields*: You might wish to take advantage of the other fields available to you. Added author can be used for a well-known illustrator or joint author. Added title can be used if there are two equal titles. Use the series field if you want to trace a series or else use the added title field.

Figure 4–4 Author Search Results

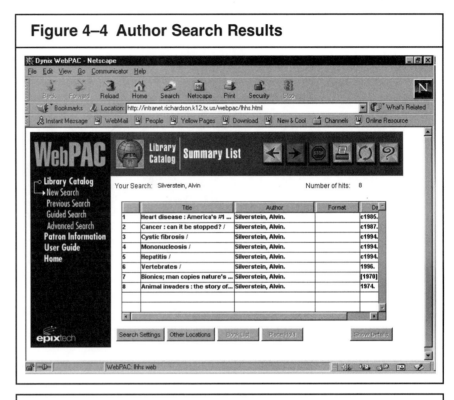

Figure 4–5 Title Search Results

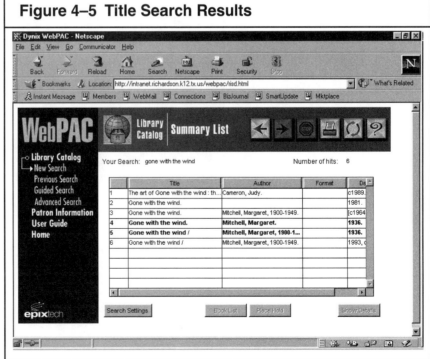

Figure 4–6 Subject Search Results

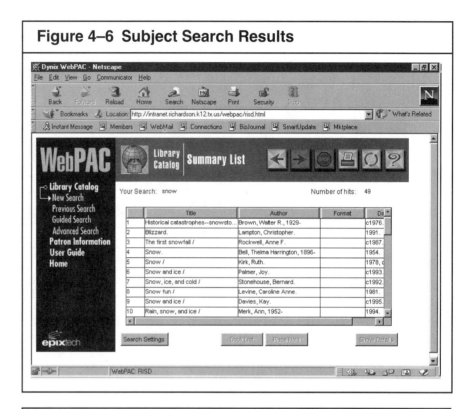

Figure 4–7 Keyword Results. Notice the Number of Hits from a Keyword Search Versus a Subject Search

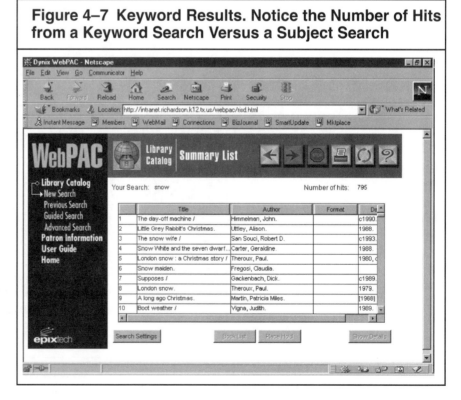

Other basic cataloging tips to help you with the input of your records:

- Capitalize the first word of the title and no other words except proper names.
- Abbreviate a long publisher's name ("Harcourt" for "Harcourt Brace Jovanovich").
- When no publication date is given, use [s.n.:s.l.].
- If the book pages are not numbered, you can put 1 v. unp.

The catalog will then allow you to search the information in a variety of ways (see Figure 4–3). Familiarize yourself with the types of results from each kind of search. Pictured here are an author, title, subject, and keyword search (Figures 4–4 through 4–7). Note the difference in results between a subject (Figure 4–6) and keyword search (Figure 4–7) using the same search term.

ELECTRONIC VS. CARD SHELFLIST

Many older libraries have well-maintained shelflists, whereas many new ones have only electronic ones. You might be in a position to decide whether to continue using your card shelflist or not. If you do, shelflist cards are simple to type or you could print a card from your computer record. Many automated systems are programmed to print a catalog card for you with everything in the right place.

If you decide to have only an electronic shelflist, you can print out a hard copy to refer to when necessary.

TIP: Shelflists are in order by Dewey call number.

TIP: You might want to give a book a special designation but still file it within a larger section. For example, you could mark a book's spine to show that it is a short story collection, and file it in the regular fiction section. Genre stickers are available through library supply companies.

HOW ARE BOOKS ARRANGED ON THE SHELVES?

Books with Dewey call numbers are arranged in numerical order according to call number. Fiction is arranged in alphabetical order by author.

The key to the arrangement of books on the shelf is accessibility. Make everything as easy to get to as possible. This means making sure everything is in its assigned place.

Nonfiction books are filed by their Dewey call numbers, then alphabetically by author's last name. For example:

370	371	371.4	372	372	373.7	373.72
B	R	C	E	F	G	L

Special collections are shelved in a separate section of the library, but they are still in order by either Dewey number or author's last name. For example, reference books are in a separate section but are still in numerical order.

AUDIOVISUAL MATERIALS

ARE AUDIOVISUAL ITEMS CATALOGED THE SAME AS BOOKS?

Electronic cataloging has simplified cataloging audiovisual items, but there are some subtle differences to an audiovisual record. You will want to use the same criteria for call numbers and subject headings as for books so these materials will appear when you or the patron searches the catalog and you can find them easily on your shelves.

Be aware of these differences while inputting records for audiovisual items:

- Special codes must be put into a record for an audiovisual item. Find out how to edit those codes for your system.
- Usually there is not an author's name.
- The title field has a General Materials Designation or gmd in brackets. This refers to the format of the item, such as [video recording].
- The physical description includes the items in the set, such as "1 box: 2 filmstrips, 2 tapes, teacher's guide."
- The publisher and date of publication are difficult to find; try to keep order information with the item until it is processed to help with the copy information.

IS CLASSIFICATION FOR BOOKS AND AUDIOVISUAL ITEMS THE SAME?

The classification used is generally the same for audiovisual items and for books. An appropriate Dewey number is needed. It is helpful to add a designation to show format. The simplest are the best. Some examples are:

FS—filmstrip
V—video
S—slides

C—cassette
R—record
CD—compact disc
CS—computer software
F—film
FL—filmloop
G—game
LD—laser disc
MF—microform
T—transparency

HOW ARE AUDIOVISUAL MATERIALS ARRANGED ON THE SHELF?

One method is to integrate books and audiovisual media on the shelf. The problem with this system, however, is that different packaging results in an inefficient use of space.

Another method is to store audiovisual materials by type. For example, all filmstrips are together, all videos are together, and so on. These collections are further divided by Dewey call number or are in alphabetical order by title.

The most widely used method is to house audiovisual materials together by Dewey call number. This system is easy for schools that restrict usage of audiovisual materials to teachers. All audiovisual materials can be stored in one area and monitored.

TIP: If you subscribe to an online magazine index, do not throw away your old Readers' Guides or other print indexes in case your computers go down or all workstations become occupied.

INDEXES, REPRINTS, AND DATABASES

WHAT INDEXES ARE MOST USEFUL IN A SCHOOL LIBRARY?

If magazine articles are to be used for research, they must be accessible by subject. Indexes provide this access and you must decide if you are going to offer this service in a print or an electronic format. All the following can be ordered from H. W. Wilson:

- *Children's Magazine Guide*: indexes the titles found most often in elementary school media centers. The format is similar to adult indexes, but with larger type and easier to read entries.
- *Abridged Readers' Guide to Periodical Literature*: indexes titles found most often in middle schools and high schools. Most school media centers subscribe to all of the magazines indexed in the *Abridged Readers' Guide*.

- *Readers' Guide to Periodical Literature*: larger in scope than *Abridged Readers' Guide*; usually found in public libraries and large high school libraries with good budgets.

WHAT OTHER SERVICES OFFER MAGAZINE AND NEWSPAPER INDEXING AND ARTICLES?

More and more magazine indexing services are available on the Internet, leaving fewer services in print or on CD-ROM.

- CD-ROM: Infotrac and Wilsonline are services that offer indexes on CD-ROM. The actual articles are available on microform, CD-ROM, or hard copy.
- Microfilm/microfiche: Some companies reprint both complete magazines and newspapers as well as selected articles onto microfilm or microfiche. You can have back issues of magazines for a relatively small cost on microfilm, which takes up much less room than bound periodicals. You will need a microfilm or microfiche reader and a printer.
- Online subscriptions services: Some services offer an online subscription to their index. Some include summaries and full-text articles. Some of the most popular are: SIRS (Social Issues Research Service), Gale, ProQuest, Electric Library, and EBSCO. Many newspapers are online free of charge. You will need a printer and supplies in addition to the computer and the networking capabilities.

VERTICAL FILES

WHAT GOES INTO A VERTICAL FILE?

A vertical file is usually a filing cabinet devoted to material of interest to a particular library. You can collect pamphlets, pictures, newspaper and magazine articles, leaflets, and other publications that will benefit your school population. Many of these materials have information found nowhere else. Often the material is free (or inexpensive), does not require cataloging, and takes up little space. Local history, school publications, or articles on school activities are materials kept in a vertical file. You might wish to keep materials related to a recurring unit.

TIP: Publishers are a good source for posters, calendars, and information on authors.

Figure 4–8 Form Letter to Request Free Materials

Letterhead

Date

Dear Sir or Madam,
Please send the following materials, which appeared as free upon request in the publication __("Free & Inexpensive Materials")__.
If there is a charge, please advise before sending. Thank you for your assistance.

_____

_____

_____
                    (name of material)
Sincerely,

R. Brown
Library/Media Specialist

HOW ARE VERTICAL FILE MATERIALS SELECTED?

Find subjects and choose materials or topics teachers assign to their classes. Find out also what subjects your teachers are personally interested in, such as travel, tax information, hobbies, and so on. Use any curriculum guides or bibliographies you have, and choose materials that are timely and up to date. Finally, listen to the students—find out what their interests are. Sources of free and inexpensive materials are listed in Appendix G.

HOW ABOUT ORDERING VERTICAL FILE MATERIAL?

Some material will come to you without ordering, such as clippings or mailings. Most other material can be requested easily. Use a form letter with a blank for the name of the requested item. Then a clerk, volunteer, or student helper can fill in the blanks and mail the letter (or send the request as e-mail).

WHAT HAPPENS WHEN THE MATERIAL ARRIVES?

Decide whether you will keep the material or not. You do not have to keep anything that will not enhance your collection.

Property-stamp the item if the stamp does not interfere with any information. Put the material into a file folder. If the source of the information is not on the material, write it on the folder. If

TIP: Updating your vertical file master list is easy if it is kept in a computer file. Then when an addition or withdrawal is made, a new list can be printed out.

there is not a subject in the vertical file for the item, create a new one.

File folders in alphabetical order. Then make a master list of subjects found in the vertical file. This typed list can be posted on or near the vertical file. Some media specialists put the subjects on cards and keep a card file close to the vertical file.

HOW ARE VERTICAL FILE MATERIALS CHECKED OUT?

Decide if vertical file materials will be used only in the media center or if they can be checked out. If you decide to check this material out, find a system that works easily for you.

A procedure commonly used is to put generic records into the computer saying "Vertical File Material" and place the corresponding bar code onto a large brown envelope. When a student wants to check out a file folder from the vertical file, it is placed inside the brown envelope and scanned. A pocket can hold the date due card or the date can be stamped directly onto the envelope.

HOW IS A SUBJECT HEADING ASSIGNED TO A VERTICAL FILE ITEM?

Assign a subject heading that describes as closely as possible the content of the entire item. Try to use the same subject headings that are most common in your collection, or use subject headings with the same terminology that students and others use when requesting information. A vertical file index can serve as a source for subject headings, especially if you use it to order material.

CIRCULATION

PROCEDURES FOR PRINT MATERIALS

WHAT LENGTH OF TIME IS BEST FOR BOOK LOANS?

Decide what is best for your situation. A two-week check-out period is used by many libraries, but you might feel that a longer or shorter time is better for you. First graders might need only a week's circulation, while a high school might have a large enough collection to allow a three- or four-week loan period. You could have such a large incidence of overdues that a longer period would be beneficial to your students.

Faculty and administration are usually allowed either a longer circulation period or an indefinite time period in which to return the books. Not only will this reduce paperwork for you, it is good PR.

HOW ARE BOOKS CHECKED OUT?

Many kinds of circulation systems can be used, from simple self-check out to totally computerized. Use the system that works best for your situation or the best you can afford. Any of these systems can be adapted if an automated system is in place.

> **Total Self-Check:** The student signs his name on the card with an identifying code, such as a room number. He then stamps the preset due date on the card and on a "date due" slip in the book and places the card in a designated place. Later someone places the cards in a file, ordered either by date and name or by homeroom.
> **Partial Self-Check:** The student signs her name and room number on the card. She then picks up a card on which the date due has already been stamped. Cards are later gathered and filed. (This is a good system if students tend to tamper with the date stamp.)
> **Total Library Check:** The student presents his library card prepared by the library. A staff person uses the library card to check out via a charging system. A date due card is put in the book with the date due already stamped on it. Sometimes the students keep their own cards or the cards are kept in a file in the library.
> **Computerized System:** Specific procedures vary with the kind of system. Generally, a bar code placed on the book is read by a light wand and checked out to a student who

is in the library's database. The student's identifying bar code is kept either on a Rolodex at the desk or on her library/ID card. Then the due date is communicated in a variety of ways: a date due card in a pocket, a sticker on the front cover, or a printed receipt given to the student.

If you are considering installing or upgrading an automated library system, write down the functions you want the system to perform and make sure the system you choose will perform those functions. The advantages of an automated library system are accuracy of recordkeeping, time saved in everyday activities, and ease of collecting statistics. The disadvantages are cost, time of converting from system to system, and the potential consequences of computer malfunction.

Most systems have representatives you can contact or manuals that explain the specifics of particular systems. Vendors have services to help you prepare your databases.

ARE REFERENCE BOOKS AND PERIODICALS EVER CIRCULATED?

Many libraries choose not to allow check out of reference books such as encyclopedias, dictionaries, atlases, and almanacs. Some check out materials on an overnight basis. Some limit check out of reference materials to teachers only. Decide which material, if any, will be available for check out, for how long, and to whom.

Most school libraries check out only back issues of periodicals for a limited period. Decide what can be checked out, if anything, and how long you will allow those materials to remain out of the library. You might want to adopt a lenient check-out policy for teachers or develop a periodical routing service.

If you circulate reference materials or periodicals, use the system that works best for you and the students. The same system you use for books can be used for these materials, or a special form can be used; for example, at the time someone checks out a magazine, the name and date of the magazine is filled in, the card signed by the student, and the form filed under the date due.

If you want to use the computer to check out periodicals, you can set up some general records using either the name of the periodical or simply "Magazines." You can then attach bar codes to an envelope, a canvas bag, or any other device that can be used over again.

> **TIP:** It is becoming harder to justify obtaining a print set of encyclopedias every year because computer formats are available. You might be able to request more budget to acquire encyclopedias and other reference materials that can be checked out to teachers on a permanent basis as the print sources they have in their classrooms become obsolete.

Figure 5–1 Overdue Notice

OVERDUE NOTICE

TO:

ROOM:

DATE:

The following items are seriously overdue from the Library/Media Center. If your books are not returned, a call will be made to your parents and your name will be given to the principal.

_____

_____

_____

Thank you for returning these items immediately.

Procedure for Routing Periodicals

1. Type lists of teachers who want to see certain periodicals. You will need to have more than one list since not all teachers want or need to see all journals.
2. Run off copies of the lists.
3. Clip the appropriate list of names to the front cover.
4. Each person checks off his name when finished.
5. He then sends the journal to the next person on the list.
6. The last person returns the journal to the library.

TIP: Advertise the fact that fine money will go for a specific purpose that will benefit the students.

WHAT IF A TEACHER WANTS A PERIODICAL EVERY MONTH WHEN IT COMES IN?

Decide if newly arrived professional periodicals should be routed to teachers. Periodicals used by teachers and students, such as *Time*, *Newsweek*, *Good Housekeeping*, and *People*, are usually left in the library. Professional journals, such as *English Journal*, are commonly routed to teachers upon their arrival. Routing gives you the opportunity to meet the teachers in your building when you ask if they wish to be placed on a routing list.

HOW ARE OVERDUES HANDLED?

Make your overdue policy known from the very beginning. Automated systems are a great time-saver where overdue notices are concerned. The system can generate the notices at a predetermined time, but if you are the one to set up these time periods, you will need to decide whether you want to do notices every day, once a week, or at the end of the semester. You need a procedure for second and third notices, too, and one for a book that is still out after a third notice. After so many computer-generated forms, you might want to have a final notice that looks different and more official (see Figure 5–1).

SHOULD FINES BE CHARGED?

If you feel that you will get results by charging fines, do so. Some library media specialists believe that fines are the only way to get overdue material in. Others believe that fines do no good one way or the other. By knowing your school population, you are

```
┌─────────────────────────────────────────────────────────┐
│ Figure 5-2 Reserve Request Form                           │
├─────────────────────────────────────────────────────────┤
│                    Book Request                           │
│ Name _____ Student # _____         │
│ Title of Book _____        │
│ Author _____Call # _____         │
│ English Teacher _____         │
│   The material requested above:                           │
│   _____ has arrived and is being held until _____.    │
│   _____ is unavailable.                                   │
└─────────────────────────────────────────────────────────┘
```

the best judge of whether fines will help you with overdues or not. Some libraries use fine money as a source of income.

WHAT SHOULD BE DONE ABOUT LOST MATERIALS?

Most libraries expect students to replace any material that is lost while checked out to them. Set your policy about the replacement of lost materials before anything is lost. Some libraries charge the replacement value rather than the original purchase price. Some add a handling fee.

SHOULD BOOKS BE RENEWED?

Decide if your students will benefit from being able to renew their books or if other students should have access to the material.

WHAT HAPPENS WHEN A LIBRARY USER WANTS A BOOK THAT IS CHECKED OUT?

Automated systems make reserving a checked-out item quite easy. Once you place a reserve on the book according to system instructions, the computer will notify you when the book is checked in that there is a reserve and whom it is for. If the book shows to be in, a library staff person should check the shelves in case the book was overlooked. Many systems will not allow you to put a reserve on a book that shows to be in.

As soon as a reserved book is returned, put it in the reserve area pending notification. Use a form to notify students. Notifications can be put in teachers' mailboxes (see Figure 5–2). The reserve slip can be paper-clipped to the cover of the book or attached with a rubber band around the outside. Be sure to write the date of notification on the reserve slip or the date when you will put the book back on the shelf if it is not picked up.

When a reserved book is checked out, throw away the original request. If there are more requests for the book, tell your user that the book cannot be renewed, if that is your policy.

TIP: While books are on reserve is a good time to make a bibliography of the titles used for a particular topic. If you use a computer, you can easily update the bibliography each year.

TIP: Don't forget the libraries in your area. If you anticipate a large need for a specific subject or type of material, alert the public library so that it can reserve these materials before all of them are checked out.

WHAT IF A TEACHER WANTS TO RESERVE SEVERAL BOOKS FOR A CLASS?

Decide on a method of reserving materials so the items are clearly marked, accessible to the users in mind, and easily recorded in your statistics. Control is your primary concern when making a reserve collection. Decide how long the check-out period is or if the materials will circulate at all, as well as how long the materials should be kept in reserve.

Here are some suggested procedures for reserve collections:

1. Put all selected materials on a book cart and mark each book as "Reserve." You can simply write "Reserve" on the date due slip or use a sticker or some other mark. You might want to make a reserve card by transferring the book card information onto a different color card and holding the check-out cards in a separate file.
2. Indicate whether a book can be checked out for a specific length of time (for example, overnight) or if it must be used in the media center.
3. Count the books checked out in your circulation statistics.
4. If your circulation is on a computer, you can easily create a reserve collection or check out the books to the requesting teacher.

CIRCULATION PROCEDURES FOR AUDIOVISUAL MATERIALS AND EQUIPMENT

HOW ARE AUDIOVISUAL ITEMS CHECKED OUT?

Decide who will be able to check out audiovisual materials to use outside the library and if there is the capability to use audiovisual materials in the library. Generally, audiovisual materials are checked out for short periods of time to students. Many schools check out only to faculty and as a professional courtesy offer either an extended or indefinite check-out period. These materials usually are checked out the same way as books, with the user either signing a card or checking out with an automated system.

HOW IS AUDIOVISUAL EQUIPMENT CHECKED OUT?

Equipment Control Board: One method is to use an equipment control board or chart. Draw blocks on a bulletin board or wipe-off board or run off a chart and laminate it to keep track of equipment (see Figure 1–1). When a piece of equipment is checked out, the number on the item is placed in the block for the room number in which the equipment will be used. When the equipment is returned, the number is either removed or moved to block for the Media Center. This is a good way to keep up with high-demand equipment that is constantly in use.

Another method for daily equipment check out is to use a calendar and simply write in the teacher's name and the equipment that has been checked out. Then cross the teacher's name off when she returns it. At the end of the day, you can tell at a glance what is still out and retrieve it.

Computerized Check Out: If you have an automated system available, attach a bar code to the equipment and enter information about the equipment into the computer. This is especially good for equipment that is checked out to one person for the entire year.

Permanent Loans: There might be equipment that is kept year-round in particular teachers' rooms yet is considered library equipment. Many times all that is needed on this equipment is a record of the room number, the teacher's signature, and the serial number of the equipment. You can create an inventory control form for this purpose or maintain a spreadsheet.

HOW CAN TEACHERS RESERVE EQUIPMENT?

Hang a large laminated calendar on the wall or use a calendar for sign up. Teachers write their names, equipment requested, and date and item requested. They can see what is being used on what days and, if necessary, put down their second choices.

A reservation form can be filled out by the teacher and put in a pocket or attached directly to the equipment. Then if someone tries to check out reserved equipment, the form will indicate there is a reserve on it.

6 MAINTAINING THE COLLECTION

ROUTINE MAINTENANCE

WHEN IS A BOOK MENDED?

If you decide that a book is valuable enough to spend time and materials mending it, then do so—neatly and carefully. Highly circulated items are likely to become worn, but if you can keep books looking as good as possible, people will continue using them. A loose pocket or date slip could be glued in as soon as it is noticed. Keeping glue at the circulation desk can save steps.

HOW IS A TORN OR DIRTY PAGE MENDED?

If a page is torn, use book tape, not Scotch tape, and tape both sides of the torn page. Allow the tape to overlap and the sticky sides to stick to each other. Then trim the excess. Avoid glue.

If a light eraser does not remove smudges, use a cleaning powder such as Absorene or a document cleaning pad purchased from a supplier such as Demco or Gaylord. Be careful to follow directions with these products. With any cleaning tool, rub gently and avoid pressing too hard or you may damage the paper.

CAN ANYONE DO REPAIRS?

Some repairs such as replacing pages or repairing the spines of books require practice and instruction. You might want one person to do repairs so the work is uniform and consistently done. Detailed instructions are included with book repair materials available from library suppliers. Kapco is a company that specializes in book repair products and provides videotaped instructions; representatives will demonstrate how to repair and preserve books. (See Appendix D for contact information.) For a complete guide to book repair procedures, consult Kenneth Lavender's *Book Repair: A How-To-Do-It Manual for Librarians, 2nd ed.* (Neal-Schuman, 2001).

If one person is designated to do repairs, a mending slip placed in the pocket of the book will inform the repairer what mending is needed (see Figure 6–1). While the book is being mended, file its circulation card in a special place so you will know where the book is. If someone asks for the book, you can flag it and notify him when it is ready to check out.

Figure 6–1 Checklist for Repairs

> **MENDING SLIP**
>
> Title
> Bar code
> Cover
> Pocket
> Replace pages
> Spine label
> Bindery
> Withdrawal
> Torn page
>   page no. _____
> Erasures
>   page no. _____
> Other

HOW ARE VERTICAL FILE MATERIALS MENDED?

These materials are not usually worth mending. If the item is to be kept and used over a period of time, you might want to laminate it to prolong its life.

Lamination can be done with a heat method, or you can buy clear adhesive plastic and carefully lay it on the front and back of the item.

WHEN IS A BOOK REBOUND?

If you decide that a book is valuable enough to spend money rebinding it, do so unless a new book is cheaper or easier to get. Consider these questions, however, before rebinding a book: Is the book out of print? Is it still needed? Is the book clean? Are any pages missing or torn? Are the pages brittle? Are the inner margins one inch wide? (The pages need room to be trimmed.) Are there any full-spread illustrations that will be spoiled by page trimming? Has the book been rebound once already? (Usually the inner margins are trimmed too much in rebinding for books to be rebound a second time.)

HOW DO YOU PREPARE BOOKS FOR BINDING?

Follow the binding company's instructions for preparing books to be rebound. The binding company might ask you to place bindery slips in each book and to enclose an alphabetical list of the books shipped. You should remove any circulation cards and file them, and remove the dust jackets and mylar covers and save them.

WHAT HAPPENS WHEN BOOKS COME BACK FROM THE BINDERY?

Prepare the books to go on the shelf. Check the invoice against the titles returned. If there are books that were not rebound, decide if these should be kept in their worn condition or discarded. Return any circulation cards to the books. Property-stamp and type new pockets. Replace the dust jackets and Mylar covers as appropriate. Send the purchase order and invoice to be paid.

WHAT ABOUT PLASTIC-BINDING PAPERBACKS?

You may have some paperbacks of value and plastic binding is a good way to preserve these materials. Books available only in paperback, donations, or high-demand items are good candidates for plastic binding. Most companies that are in the library binding business offer plastic binding services.

WHAT CAN YOU DO TO PROLONG THE LIFE OF LIBRARY EQUIPMENT?

Most equipment should be cleaned and checked once a year. Equipment will last longer and perform better if properly maintained, just as your car lasts longer with regular maintenance.

A logical time of year to do this regular maintenance is during the summer. Your school district might have a service center, or a regional service center could provide maintenance service. If not, check for a locally available commercial service.

Making minor repairs yourself will save time and keep the equipment from being unavailable. Required maintenance can include changing lamps and simple cleaning. Use the manual that comes with each piece of equipment for thorough details on repairs and maintenance. Keep a dust cover on equipment when it is not in use.

> **Changing Lamps:** When a piece of equipment is purchased, note what lamp it requires and be sure to have replacements on hand. When replacing a lamp, unplug the machine so you do not risk hurting yourself or the machine. Locate the position of the lamp and, using a cloth, gently pull it out. Be sure to replace it with the right size. If the equipment is older and you do not know what size you need, call the manufacturer or check the manual if you have one.
>
> **Cleaning Lenses:** If a projector produces unclear images, you might have a dirty lens. Clean lenses by gently wiping with a nonsilicon-type lens tissue, special lens cleaner, or a soft, lint-free cloth. Never touch a lens with your fingers or blow on it. Canned air can be used.

Cleaning Tape Recorders: You can prolong the life of audio and videocassette recorders by routinely cleaning the tape heads. This can be done by purchasing a tape cleaning cassette and running it in the machine the same way you would play any tape. An alternative is to use a cleaning solution specifically for tape recorders and a cotton swab, being careful to apply it only to the tape heads.

Troubleshooting: If equipment is not working, the first thing to check is whether the item or extension cord is plugged in. Next, are all the switches turned on? Are all cables and cords properly attached?

Safeguards: When using any audiovisual equipment, always observe the following basic safety precautions:

- Unplug the machine when not in use. To disconnect it from an electrical outlet, pull on the plug; do not yank the cord.
- Do not operate equipment with damaged cords.
- Do not let cords hang over the edge of tables or counters or touch hot surfaces.
- Do not operate equipment near water.
- Do not force anything.
- Let the machine cool before moving it. Let the fan cool the motor before turning it off.

For more information, consult *Managing Public Access Computers: A How-To-Do-It Manual for Librarians* by Donald Barclay (Neal-Schuman, 2000).

INVENTORY

WHEN SHOULD YOU DO INVENTORY?

Many librarians do inventory at the end of the school year. Depending on individual needs and time structures, however, inventory can also be done at the beginning or in the middle of the year. If your library is automated, inventory can be done easily anytime. If you operate under a manual system, inventory is easiest when all materials are in place, i.e., either before opening or after closing the library for the year.

WHY DO INVENTORY?

An inventory gives you the opportunity to find out what is missing so it can be replaced or deleted from the total book count. Many librarians use inventory as an opportunity to learn the collection. It is also a good time to find out which materials need mending, rebinding, or repairs.

How Do You Do an Inventory?

There are two main types of inventory, manual and automated. Even with an automated system, you may wish to do a manual inventory, operating from a printout. If your library has been through a renovation or some other major event, a manual inventory will help you make sure everything is in order.

> **Manual Inventory:** Here are the steps you should follow when doing inventory manually:
> * Read the shelves and get all the materials in order.
> * Take one drawer from the shelflist catalog at a time to the corresponding shelf of books in the library or a portion of the printout. Look at the first entry in the shelflist. Check the shelf to see if the book is on the shelf. Continue through the entire list. If the book is not on the shelf, look around. If it is close by, reshelve it.
> * If the book cannot be located, mark the entry. In pencil, note "missing" and the year. If the book was missing after the previous inventory, process the item as lost. If the book was previously missing but found in a later inventory, it might need to be input into the computer again.
> * After all the shelves have been read, look in other sources, such as teachers' rooms, the principal's office, or the book room, for materials noted as missing.
> * Remove and set aside any materials that appear worn or in need of repair.
>
> **Automated Inventory:** If the records are in order, follow directions for the system you have. General guidelines are:
> * Read the shelves and get all materials in order.
> * Pass the inventory scanner over each book.
> * Download the information into the computer. The program will then search for missing books.
> * Decide which missing items are to be replaced or deleted from the collection.

To do an equipment inventory, prepare a master list of serial numbers using the maintenance data. Check the master list against the equipment, noting the condition (life expectancy) of equipment.

MATERIALS SELECTION

HOW DO YOU DECIDE WHAT TO PURCHASE?

Whatever you purchase is bought for the teachers, students, and administrators who will use the materials. Here are some things to consider:

- academic philosophy
- curriculum
- reading interest levels
- format
- balance
- intellectual freedom

In deciding what to purchase, you must balance the needs of everyone. Get as much input as possible from everyone who is served by the library, especially students. You will also have many other influences on your selection of materials. For instance, district and school philosophy will guide you. Know what the definitive guidelines are for both the school and the district. These guidelines represent community input in your selection. If there are no guidelines, formulate a philosophy for your own school and, if possible, help create one for the entire district.

Most purchases reinforce the school curriculum. The media center is an extension of the classroom, so your goal is to enhance and supplement what teachers teach and what students learn.

In every elementary, middle, and high school, students are on varying reading and interest levels. Provide a range of levels so the library will have something for everyone.

Deciding between print and nonprint materials requires an understanding of learning and teaching styles. A variety of media will ensure that all styles will be accommodated.

The balance of the collection is critical. Not only should the collection be balanced in terms of the population served, there should also be a balance of subjects. Represent all subject areas and genres.

Think in terms of intellectual freedom. All viewpoints must be represented in the materials chosen for the media center. Be especially mindful of recent cultural changes in the school community, students for whom English is a second language, and students with different learning capabilities.

WEEDING

WHY WEED?

Old, obsolete, worn, and inappropriate materials can get in the way of library users' finding new, current, and appropriate materials they need. Materials that are worn and old can give the media center a drab and careless appearance. Sometimes valuable storage room is taken up by these old materials, too. Finally, keeping obsolete materials to increase the collection count could keep you from getting additional funds to update your collection.

WHO DOES THE WEEDING?

You are the best person to weed. You know the collection and the needs of your users better than anyone. However, it is advisable and customary for teachers to assist with the weeding for their specialty areas. To encourage teachers to participate, remind them that new materials are ordered to fill gaps in the collection left by withdrawal of old materials.

WHEN SHOULD THE LIBRARY MEDIA SPECIALIST WEED?

Every year. If you wait until much of the collection is worn out, you will have to discard such a large amount that everyone will become alarmed. Teachers become used to the old material and might want an explanation for their favorite material being thrown away.

Weed throughout the year as you are actively working with the collection. Keeping a record of which items in the collection were weeded, and when, will help you. If time permits, weed while you do inventory.

WHAT SHOULD BE WEEDED?

Materials with old, out-of-date, and incorrect information should be weeded. You should be careful to update the science technology, medicine, and geography sections. Be sure to keep especially up to date on drug and health information. Use these guidelines as suggestions: encyclopedias—no older than 5 years; dictionaries—no older than 12 or 15 years; atlases—no older than 10 years;

almanacs—keep only current editions in the reference section (remove others from inventory count and use for instruction).

Be aware of biased, condescending, patronizing, or stereotyping materials. These should go.

Worn-out or badly damaged materials will make your library look dingy. Look for these signs: brittle, yellow, dirty pages; ragged bindings; poor quality pictures; loose or missing sections; audiovisual kits with missing pieces; damaged audiovisual materials such as broken tapes or filmstrips with torn sprocket holes.

Do not keep unused materials. One rule of thumb is if the item has not been used in five years, consider withdrawing it. Keep in mind, however, there are many useful items that are not frequently circulated. Finally, textbooks and supplementary texts do not need to take up valuable room on the library shelves.

WHAT SHOULD NOT BE DISCARDED?

Some materials are unique to your collection or are "timeless." As these become worn, rebind and mend to keep them in as good a condition as possible.

Do not discard: classics, unless specific items are too worn to carry on the shelves; local and state history, unless there are new copies to replace the old; school annuals and other campus publications; materials that do not change rapidly, such as fairy tales, fiction, biography, fine arts, sports (except for rule books and statistics), poetry and literature, languages, and religion.

HOW DO YOU DISCARD BOOKS?

Here is a system many librarians use:

1. Remove titles from the computer system and from any other lists.
2. Stamp "discard" or "withdrawn" on the books on the title page, the front, and the back. Anywhere there is a property stamp, stamp "discard."
3. Destroy the item. (Be sure to check the district policy on discarding. Some districts require complete destruction or allow items to be sent elsewhere.)
4. Do a withdrawals report at the end of the year.

WHAT ABOUT MATERIALS PURCHASED WITH FEDERAL FUNDS?

Pay special attention to the rules concerning forms and reports that must be filed on items purchased with federal funds. Usually a school district policy concerns disposal of these items, although there is normally no difference in procedures, only in reporting.

WHEN SHOULD MATERIALS BE WEEDED?

General Reference: Print encyclopedias might not need to be replaced frequently depending on the availability of online encyclopedias. Just realize and emphasize to your users that much of the information will be outdated in old print sets. Bibliographical sources need to be considered for weeding on the same basis. Yearbooks and almanacs should be updated as superseded.

000s: Computer materials change rapidly with the technology, so replacement is required often. Bibliographies are seldom useful after ten years from date of copyright.

100s: Self-help, psychology, and guidance materials need to be reviewed for dated pictures and concepts. Most unscholarly works are useless after ten years.

200s: Philosophical and religious materials should be reviewed individually and as a collection to ensure that as many points of view as possible are represented.

300s: Certain subject areas need constant revision, and others should be weeded very carefully and infrequently. Basic sources on customs and volumes of folklore will probably need to be removed only because of poor physical condition. Depending on the curriculum, historical coverage of economics, communication, transportation, politics, and education can be maintained. Career materials should be discarded after five years. Be particularly aware of qualifications discrepancies in materials dealing with career preparation. Review of audiovisual sources for dated dress and mannerisms is especially important.

400s: Depending on the size and use of the collection, old grammar materials and foreign language sources should be examined for dated examples and illustrations. Dictionaries can change in terms of what words are included, especially slang words that have come into common usage. Twelve to fifteen years is the recommended replacement period for dictionaries.

500s: Unless general science works have become classics, obsolete materials should be discarded. Specific scientific areas change at different rates. Astronomy materials can become dated before botany sources. New discoveries in energy require updating works in this field more often than materials in subjects such as natural history. Many materials related to the environment are still appropriate after fifteen years, while an item about atoms could be inaccurate after two years.

600s: Many of the concerns identified for the 500s apply to the 600s as well. Materials on medicine, radio, television, industry, space exploration, and automobiles become dated rapidly. Books in popular areas such as pets, crafts, and cooking tend to be used often and might need to be replaced because of their condition.

700s: This section often includes collections of handsomely illustrated sources on music and the fine arts that might be irreplaceable. Sources that are heavily used should be considered for replacement or, as is often the case, rebinding. Materials on certain hobbies might need updating. Use patterns should play a role in determining what needs updating. Sources on various sports should be current, with duplicate copies available.

800s: Literary history should seldom be discarded unless drastic curriculum changes are made. Decisions about collections versus individual works of major and minor poets, novelists, and playwrights should be made according to curriculum needs and use patterns. Keep works by local authors.

900s: Many geography and travel materials tend to become dated quickly. Except for items that have become classics, geography and travel materials that are over ten years old should be considered for removal or replacement. Historical materials should be examined for use patterns as well as bias. The collection should contain a range of materials on all historical periods and be examined for coverage. Materials once purchased for coverage can be replaced with items of better quality. Keep atlases and geographic material for no more than ten years.

Biography: Unless a subject is of permanent interest or importance, discard these books when the demand wanes. Keep those that are outstanding in content or style as long as they are useful.

Fiction and "Easy" Books: Use patterns greatly influence the review of fiction collections. Materials popular one year will sit on the shelves at other times. Duplicates once needed might no longer be appropriate. Replacement of popular worn items must be considered. Rebinding of out-of-print items can be an option if they fill a specific curriculum need or reading interest.

Periodicals: Do not keep longer than a year unless indexed. If indexed, keep no longer than the oldest index or for five to eight years, depending on use. For magazines, take out the oldest year in the collection. These materials can then be cut up and put in the vertical or picture file.

Vertical File: As new materials are added, check to see if any new item makes an old item obsolete. If so, pull and discard the old item.

Audiovisual Materials: The same general guidelines apply to audiovisual materials that were discussed for books. Check for missing pieces in audiovisual kits, damaged materials such as broken videocassettes, timeliness of materials, and use in the curriculum. Remember to check for dated dress and dialog.

CHALLENGED MATERIALS

The Library Bill of Rights states that everyone must have access to materials, regardless of origin, age, background, or views. An interpretation of this document for school libraries has been developed and is in Appendix N. This document further establishes that materials will not be labeled by age or grade and that children do not need permission from parents or teachers to check out certain materials. Nonetheless, there is a history of challenges to library materials by parents, community members, and even teachers and administrators. Regardless of the material, the procedures for handling these complaints are the same.

Have a written policy in place that has been voted on by the school board. If such a policy does not exist, draft one for your principal's approval at your school at the earliest possible time and begin procedures for having it adopted districtwide.

When a material is challenged, ask the person making the challenge to fill out a form for reconsideration of the material (see Figure 6–2). Calmly explain the process that will be taken to handle the challenged material.

When the written form has been returned, check to make sure it is filled out completely. Proceed only if the form is filled out and if the person making the challenge has read or viewed the challenged item in its entirety.

Choose people to serve on a committee to review the complaint. The committee makeup should be designated in your policy and should include a teacher, a librarian, an administrator, a community representative, and a library administrator from another district.

Your responsibility to the committee is to provide background

Figure 6–2 Request for Reconsideration Form

REQUEST FOR RECONSIDERATION OF INSTRUCTIONAL MATERIALS

Title _____   Medium:

Author _____   Audiovisual Resource   _____

Producer _____   Book   _____

Name of Person Initiating Request _____   Periodical   _____

Supplemental Material   _____

Other   _____

Telephone _____ Address _____

City _____ Zip Code _____

Complaint Represents:

_____ Self

_____ Organization   Name of Organization _____

1. Did you review or preview the entire work? _____

2. What do you believe is the theme or purpose of this work? _____
_____

3. Please state nature of objection (be specific; cite pages or other identifying factors). _____
_____

4. What do you feel might be the result of using this material? _____
_____

5. What do you feel should be done with the material in question? _____
_____

6. Are you aware of the teacher's purpose in using this work? _____
_____

7. In its place, what selection of equal value would you recommend? _____
_____

8. Comments _____
_____

Signature _____   Date _____

Used with permission of the Richardson Independent School District.

information on the material, including professional reviews, information regarding the status of the challenged material at other libraries, and any other information pertinent to the committee's task. The committee then makes its decision, which is forwarded to the school board or superintendent. The challenged material should remain in circulation until a decision is made.

You can seek help with challenged materials from publishers, professional organizations, other librarians, and publications such as the *Intellectual Freedom Newsletter* (available from ALA's Office for Intellectual Freedom). Often the challenge will be dropped because the form is never filled out and returned. Nevertheless, the best way to handle challenged materials is to be prepared ahead of time with a written and approved policy. Regardless of who the complainant is, whether parent, teacher, principal, or superintendent, you will be prepared to hand that person a form to fill out.

Most procedures for filing complaints about materials are designed for print or audiovisual materials. Complaints about online resources are generally trickier. Go through the process for filing complaints when the question is about objectionable Web sites linked to your library's Web site. If all the parties in your process agree that the site is objectionable and you have filtering software, remove the link. Emphasize that the purpose for computers at school is for research and not for recreation.

7 HIRING AND WORKING WITH STAFF

The library media specialist is considered part of the faculty. In addition to an undergraduate degree, a graduate degree and experience in education are considered necessary qualifications for a library media specialist.

You also have a team of people to help you in the library. You might have a full-time hired staff or you might have volunteers, but by creating a team spirit, you can organize a group to help you run and maintain the library in the optimum way. Staff and volunteers are most comfortable when jobs are well defined. If job descriptions have not been written down previous to your arrival, have staff write their job descriptions and then together fine-tune them until all of you are satisfied. Involving the staff in policies that affect them gives them a sense of pride and control in their environment, increasing morale. This can be a first step in keeping communication open.

Schedule regular meetings or sit-down sessions to establish a working relationship that benefits the library environment. Faculty teams have regular planning sessions; your staff will appreciate planning the library operation, too.

First of all, let's take a look at your job description:

PROFESSIONALS AND PARAPROFESSIONALS

The library media specialist has the following professional duties:

- Develops goals and objectives for the library media center (LMC) program cooperatively with teachers, administrators, and students. Consults and plans with teachers on the appropriate use and convenient scheduling of materials for classroom instruction.
- Works with teachers by recommending and planning for user needs.
- Plans with administrators, teachers, and students, individually and in groups, for effective use of LMC materials and facilities.
- Provides leadership in evaluating and selecting materials and equipment for purchase.

- Assumes responsibility for processing and organizing all LMC materials and equipment.
- Encourages student use of materials to satisfy class assignments.
- Functions as an active member of the faculty by accepting teaching responsibilities in student use of LMC materials and as a resource person in classroom activities.
- Assists in the design and production of teaching materials not available from commercial sources.
- Informs the faculty of available community resources by maintaining a file that includes a listing of field trips, persons with special expertise, community activities and celebrations.
- Acquires materials not available in the school LMC through interlibrary loan.
- Provides user guidance in reading, viewing, and listening.
- Prepares subject area or topic bibliographies incorporating all types of materials.
- Assists teachers in integrating media (including the Internet and other electronic information sources) with instructional assignments.
- Maintains appropriate lines of communication with the district library media director.
- Incorporates district policies and procedures into the campus LMC program.
- Plans activities to stimulate student and teacher use of LMC materials and facilities.
- Maintains schedules for instructional television programs and encourages the use of video programs for educational purposes.
- Keeps systematic records and data so that program efficiency can be evaluated.
- Notifies users of new materials, equipment, and services on a regular basis.
- Collects information about user interests and needs and routes relevant information and materials regarding those interests and needs to appropriate groups.
- Plans and directs the activities of the school library aides, clerks, volunteers, and student assistants.
- Leads technological plans and encourages schoolwide respect for copyright law.
- Develops a useful, relevant professional collection.
- Acquires materials that will provide options in instructional methods for students.

HOW DO YOU SELECT SUPPORT STAFF?

Look for:

- dependability
- interest in library work
- enjoyment of children
- technical skill

Look for people who will be part of the media center and school team. When you are interviewing a candidate, know the district rules and guidelines for hiring aides. Prepare questions in advance; if you are prepared, you will be more at ease. Put candidates at ease, too; a little casual conversation helps.

Be specific with your questions. Ask how candidates have handled particular situations in the past. This gives good clues as to how they will perform in similar situations in the future. Describe the job, days and hours required, and benefits in detail. Also describe what your expectations will be of the person who gets the job.

You cannot, by law, ask questions about any personal data, such as family concerns, not related to the job.

WHAT ARE THE DUTIES OF SUPPORT STAFF?

Support staff free the library media specialist for professional duties. They perform a wide variety of tasks, ranging from circulation to book repair. There are three different levels of support staff.

Paraprofessionals: Paraprofessionals usually have a college education and technical training so they can do more than clerical tasks. These staff members can help with computer support, individualized instruction, and other special tasks.

Clerical Staff: Clerical staff frequently include people with business or secretarial experience. In addition to computer data entry, they help shelve, maintain order, and handle circulation routines.

Technicians: Technicians have media production or computer skills. They help keep equipment in good condition, take photographs, produce graphics, and perform other technical duties. Technical assistants are familiar with library routines.

Many libraries have only one support staff person who might perform any or all of these jobs including the preparation of displays, bulletin boards, graphs, charts, and production of other instructional aids such as transparencies, audio and video tapes, worksheets, tests, or other materials.

MEDIA CLERKS AND STUDENT ASSISTANTS

SAMPLE JOB DESCRIPTION FOR A MEDIA CLERK

The duties of a media clerk include the following:

- Schedule and operate equipment for teachers and students.
- Assist with the audiotaping or videotaping of classroom or other educational experiences.
- Receive, check, and process new materials and equipment.
- Maintain equipment and materials.
- Request and schedule use of materials from the district LMC, regional education service center, or other source.
- Provide instruction and assistance in operating equipment.
- Assist teachers and students in locating, circulating, and using resources.
- Type bibliographies, letters, purchase orders, requisitions, and routine correspondence.
- Update computer catalog.
- Balance accounts.
- Organize, schedule, and circulate materials and equipment.
- Assist users in locating and using materials and equipment.
- Shelve materials returned to the LMC.
- Maintain files on materials, facilities, and personnel available from community sources.
- Work with students to maintain an orderly atmosphere.
- Repair materials and equipment.
- Help produce instructional media.
- Assist with inventory and weeding procedures.
- Keep program records.
- Maintain an attractive appearance of the LMC.

HOW DO YOU TRAIN A NEW SUPPORT STAFF PERSON?

Generally, introduce one new skill at a time to a new staff member. A checklist of skills can help you prepare your orientation and training sessions. You will have a written record of the training agenda and the person's progress. Keep notes as she progresses in case you are expected to participate in her performance evalu-

TIP: A handbook of procedures will help you train all your staff so work is done in a standard, consistent way. But writing your own handbook can seem like an overwhelming task! Cooperate with other district personnel to produce a uniform manual for all schools in the district. If there is a well-trained staff person already in place at your school, ask that person's help in writing a procedures manual. If you are anticipating a change in personnel, this process could help bridge the gap between outgoing and incoming staff.

ation. Find out what skill level the new staff person has achieved in previous experiences. If you interviewed her, you already have a feel for how skilled she may be. Approach the training process with patience and set a realistic time frame to allow the new person to learn and practice each new skill.

Here are some steps to follow:

1. Present information about the task performed, and explain why it is necessary.
2. Allow the aide to practice. Watch and provide immediate feedback.
3. Allow the aide to try the task alone, then check to see if any further instruction is needed.

Introduce the next skill only after the first task is mastered. Present skills as they are needed.

HOW ARE STUDENT ASSISTANTS SELECTED?

Look for:

- interest in library work
- dependability
- self-reliance

Selection of good student assistants is vital to the success of your program.

Students' schedules are a big factor in getting their assistance. In an elementary school, assign a student helper from each class to assist when his class is in the library. The assistant could come from a pool of students trained in an after-school program to "certify" them in equipment operation, check-out procedures, and other duties. If you have a before- or after-school day-care program that meets at your school, recruit helpers from that group if everyone is agreeable.

In secondary schools, library work might replace study hall, but a student can also be referred from an academic class by a teacher. Avoid a tug of war with teachers over students. You can recruit in study hall, but not in an academic class. Teachers and counselors can recommend students who would make good student helpers.

TIP: Students who are not academically oriented often make good library workers. Special education students can perform many tasks, and the status of their position will raise their self-image.

HOW ARE STUDENT WORKERS TRAINED?

Be sure to train all students, even returning ones, before assigning regular duties. Assigning duties to students is an individual task. Consider the students' interests, age, and abilities.

There are several ways to train students. You might train a whole group of students at one time, either before or after school, but individual on-the-job training is most common. Over a period of time, students are taught a variety of skills. Rotate tasks so everyone gets a chance to do the desirable jobs.

If you are required to document the grades you give to students, create individual units so students can learn their skills in a self-paced manner and in whatever order is needed. The lessons completed are recorded on a student's master list. After the student completes the activities, a test demonstrates mastery of the task. The skill is recorded and another topic is selected. Although this system requires a lot of time to set up, once in place the topic packets can be used indefinitely.

WHAT ARE THE DUTIES OF A STUDENT ASSISTANT?

The duties of a student assistant will depend on her age and abilities. Be careful about assigning students to work with machines that are too big for them. Students can perform all stages of the circulation process, which improves service and helps control theft. They can check out, check in, and shelve books.

Students can also help with the processing of materials. Break down the processing into its simplest parts. Students can unpack and verify contents on the packing slip, open books, check call numbers, stamp the school name, and paste pockets. If a computerized system is used, students with typing skills can enter the data. Devise a system to verify their work, such as a regularly scheduled printout or a manual check of each book and record.

Students can cut out articles previously marked by a staff member for the vertical file. They can staple together continuous pages or mount single-column items on a sheet of paper, then file them in the proper folders.

When equipment is on carts, students can deliver almost anything. Use caution, however, in allowing students to move equipment that is larger than they are. Depending on a student's age and the weight of the videotaping equipment, she can help with videotaping school activities.

Students also can help with inventory and call out information or use a computer system. Other jobs include running errands, straightening, dusting shelves, and helping make bulletin boards.

TIP: Check a student's filing by having him shelve the books so that colored strips of paper will stick out and then review with him any mistakes. Each student can use a different color.

TIP: Be sure to give students plenty of incentives and "perks" to keep them interested all year long.

Figure 7–1 Volunteer Application Form

VOLUNTEER APPLICATION FORM

Thank you for your interest in volunteering for the school library. The service that we provide to the students of this school is greatly enhanced by the efforts of volunteers like you. Because we want to provide the best for our students, we ask that you commit to a schedule and give advance notice if you are unable to work. If regularly working in the school library becomes a burden on you, please let us know so we can adjust your schedule with you.

There will be a training session on Sept. 5 at 10:00. Please make every effort to attend.

NAME:

PHONE:

CONTACT PERSON (in case of emergency:

_____ PHONE:

1. Do you have previous library experience either as a volunteer or employee?

2. List any special knowledge or skills that will help you as a library volunteer.

3. Is there a library job in which you are especially interested?

ADULT VOLUNTEERS

When using adult volunteers, match the volunteer to the task. Sources of adult volunteer workers include:

- parent groups
- businesses who adopt a school
- senior citizen groups

Adult volunteers add a worthwhile contribution to media center programs. An essential part of assigning tasks to a volunteer is knowing not only what that person is capable of doing, but what the person wants and expects to do. An initial interview can help you determine what the expectations of the volunteer are and what you can assign them that will give you and the volunteer the most satisfaction (see Figure 7–1). When you know how regularly an adult volunteer will come to the library, assign the person tasks that require the least amount of training. Since some jobs, such as book repair, are done only when the need arises, these might be good for volunteers.

SAMPLE JOB DESCRIPTION FOR VOLUNTEERS

Adult volunteers frequently assist libraries when they:

- Tell or read stories to students.
- Use story records, films, filmstrips, and tapes with students.
- Work with individuals, small groups, or large groups in the areas of subject specialization, such as demonstrating the various arts of music, painting, dance, sculpture, and drama.
- Assist in helpful, daily tasks such as processing materials, simple mending, maintaining vertical files, making displays, and circulating and reshelving materials.

Be sure to give your volunteers guidance and plenty of positive reinforcement. They need to feel they are an important part of your program and your school. Thank them for each activity. Visit during coffee breaks, introduce them to the principal and staff, send them personal thank-you letters. Recognize volunteers with a luncheon or tea periodically—perhaps twice a year.

8 DESIGNING AND USING THE FACILITY

To get the most out of your space, think of your library as you would your living room at home. Rearranging the furniture and accessories creates different moods, optimizes available space, and changes the traffic flow. Technology needs have made this aspect of running a library media center more challenging than ever. But a comfortable, welcoming environment can be achieved in the library as well as in a living room.

Your arrangement of the library must accommodate all the needs of your program including the collection, media center staff, student body, and class needs. For instance, an elementary library needs an attractive, spacious storytime area. A library with a paraprofessional staff needs to have workspace for them. Is there a way to include a television/VCR or computer in a class area so you could use a PowerPoint presentation or a video? Which way will the screen face based on the placement of the equipment? Can the furniture be arranged to accommodate the technology? Do you have areas for recreational reading? Do you need a separate computer lab? As computers are introduced to your library, they are usually done so gradually. Have an expansion plan as you increase the number of computers, with electrical outlets ready for computer installation.

> **TIP:** Planning your space? Consider:
> - student needs
> - your teaching style
> - staff
> - class needs
> - collection size and expansion
> - technology needs

CREATING MOODS

Hard vs. soft: The library can appear anywhere on the continuum between hard and soft. Most libraries have elements creating a hard effect, such as tables and chairs, computer workstations, and wooden or metal bookshelves. Some ways to soften this hard appearance and make a more inviting atmosphere are to add things like plants, carpets, curtains, and beanbag chairs.

Color: The use of color is very important in creating the kind of mood desired. Cool colors such as blue and green are associated with calm, restfulness, and passivity. Warm colors such as red, orange, and yellow are associated with excitement, cheerfulness, and energy. Up until age six or seven, children prefer reds, oranges, and yellows. There is a shift away from warm colors to a preference for blues and greens as they grow older.

Color changes the apparent size of a room. Light colors enlarge a room while darker colors make a room appear smaller. Use of a light color on the ceiling also increases the perceived size of the room. This is most useful when the library has a low ceiling or is located in the basement. If the ceiling is very high, as with some older buildings, a darker color will create a more pleasing effect. The perceived proportions of the room can be altered by painting an end wall a lighter or darker color than the surrounding walls.

Different areas of the library can be highlighted using varying colors. For example, a storyhour area can be set apart by bright colors while a quiet study area will need a cool color.

The perceived temperature of the room can also be changed through the use of color. Color absorbs light and converts it into heat. If you want to increase the temperature of a room, use brighter, darker colors, which absorb more light. If the room temperature tends to be warm, you can cool it down with lighter colors.

Lighting: Natural lighting can create impressive images, but that is not always best for libraries. Some buildings have skylights and large picture windows flooding the interior with sunlight. This is good for growing plants, but it is hard on the eyes for reading. You might need to add curtains or blinds during peak sunlight hours.

The opposite problem of too little natural light is obviously compensated for by the use of artificial lighting. In this case, light walls and white ceilings will reflect the most light and reduce glare or eyestrain.

OPEN AND CLOSED SPACES

A library needs a combination of open and private spaces. Open spaces are conducive to group interaction and are necessary for class activities. Closed or isolated spaces are preferred, even by young children, to peruse materials quietly. If your library is too small to provide adequately for these needs, the arrangement of furniture becomes crucial.

Frequently, bookshelves are lined up around the edge of the

room with the interior space filled with tables and chairs. Breaking up that interior pattern with low, freestanding bookshelves can create new spaces for individual activities, small groups, or separation of classes. Study carrels or workstations can be used to create individual study areas. When carrels are lined up in a long row, students are sitting next to each other without much privacy. Instead of a row, place them in groups of four with their backs together, separating the students from each other. Other ways of separating spaces include freestanding screens, bulletin boards or displays, and decorated cardboard boxes.

Outside windows can provide pleasing effects, especially if they look out onto a well-landscaped area or a pleasing hallway of the school. If students look into those windows when walking by, however, they distract students trying to study. You might need to partially cover these windows.

FURNISHINGS

If you want to encourage group interaction, use round tables. Rectangular tables are conducive to everyone having his own little space. If more seating is needed, avoid sofas or joined chairs. People tend to sit by themselves on sofas.

Your computers and the furniture necessary for that equipment take up a lot of room. In addition to that, you must accommodate the power supply that runs all the equipment, the network connections as you become part of a larger network, and the cords required. For security reasons, you will also want the screens facing in such a direction that you can monitor student use of the computers. All these factors can make computer arrangement awkward if not originally planned for, and you will find yourself placing large furniture in places you will not like. Find out if you can move computer drops and cable outlets and have new electrical outlets installed.

TRAFFIC FLOW

The first thing to consider in furniture arrangement is the traffic flow through the library. The best location for the circulation or check-out desk is near the door for security reasons. This is a high-mobility area requiring open space and not conducive to closed or private areas. Instead, place newspapers, paperbacks, and soft seating nearby.

Another high-traffic spot is the online catalog location. Provide space nearby for note taking, and do not crowd the area with other kinds of furniture. Analyze student usage patterns to allow room for the collaboration that naturally occurs. Decide if you want standing stations or sitting stations. It is generally convenient to locate reference materials in this same area.

You can affect the way traffic is channeled through the library by the way you arrange furniture. If there are no walls, you can create false entrances by arranging bookshelves around the imaginary perimeter of the library; leave openings in the shelves where you want students to walk. If the arrangement of the school and library dictates that students will walk through the library en route to somewhere else, you can direct that traffic to the least obstructive path by creating barriers with bookshelves, computers and other equipment, and furniture.

REARRANGING THE LIBRARY

Rearranging? Think about:
- measuring
- plotting on a grid
- traffic flow
- noisy areas vs. study areas
- costs

Rearranging the library will occur frequently as technology places more demands on the existing space. However, you do not want to constantly move furniture around trying to find the best place for it. Therefore, plan your ideas on paper before you move anything. Use grid paper and symbols for furniture. These are available in library furniture catalogs. Measure accurately and transfer to your grid. Plan for the space needed to move around the furniture; the placement of electrical outlets, doors, and other permanent fixtures; and future equipment, including computers, televisions, and screens.

By arranging on paper, you can try different plans, consult others in the building, and eventually know what to tell the people who will help you move the furniture. This is the time when you can analyze traffic flow, decide on how much cost you can afford, and determine if this will fix the problem that initiated the change in the first place. Be careful not to create any blind spots with the new arrangement.

How do you guesstimate the number of computers to include in a school library when designing or remodeling a facility? Go to www.school-library.org for Simpson's Calculator, which is a simple form to help you determine the number of computers that will provide adequate access for every grade level and academic orientation.

ELECTRONIC NEEDS

If you are anticipating major technological changes, consult with experts about computer systems, heating and cooling, electrical systems, and so on. They will know the building codes and specifications. Tell them what you need to accomplish and ask them questions with your goals in mind. Details like windows can be a huge factor in successfully achieving your goals. You might need to have a window treatment installed that will block enough sunlight to darken a room adequately to project an image.

Consider the ergonomic factors of computer desks and chairs. Make sure computers have room for ventilation. Armless swivel chairs with casters are considered the best for computer use. Computer monitors can wash out if the lighting around the screen is too harsh. Adjustable lighting is preferable for both projected images as well as high computer usage. Even the colors on walls can reflect light and be a factor in looking at computer screens. Room temperature should be kept low to protect computer equipment. You might want to have copy holders either attached to the computer or freestanding.

As teaching methods change, your facility will also undergo changes. If you are in an older building, technology will force you to constantly rethink the effectiveness of your library. Look for ideas in journals, talk to any librarian who goes through a renovation, and frequently ask your technology specialists in your school and district for suggestions specific to your building.

9 INFORMATION LITERACY

The primary mission of teacher-librarians has remained constant over the decades: teaching students how to meet their information needs. However, the palette of information tools has changed dramatically over the last few years. While this is an ever growing challenge, contact with students is the purpose of all the management and administrative chores and the most enjoyable part of the job. It is for the programming—with students directly and for students through collaboration with teachers, administrators, and parents—that all else about the library media center and its staff exist.

PROVIDING INFORMATION

HOW DO YOU HELP SOMEONE FIND ANSWERS TO QUESTIONS?

Since every reference question is a learning experience for all concerned, this becomes a very important contact. In addition to finding the information, you have an opportunity to instruct the user on the library and its resources so she will be a more independent library user.

Treat every question seriously. Try to find out exactly what information the person needs. Sometimes, knowing how the information will be used (for a report, to satisfy curiosity, for personal use, and so on) is helpful. Find out if the person has found anything independently. If not, suggest some ways to look up subjects. This could be a chance to use online resources, if available.

Direct the user to the tools or sources that can help. If your library does not have the resources to answer a particular question, call another library or access information via computer. If you have an interlibrary loan arrangement, you can get the requested information quickly. If you believe that some other community resource besides the public library has helpful information, refer the user to this resource.

HOW DO YOU HELP A STUDENT FIND SOMETHING TO READ OR VIEW?

You must draw on your special knowledge of your collection and your insight into each individual student. First of all, know your collection by using it. Read, view, and listen to as many of your items as possible. Be aware of how the variety of media complement each other.

Figure 9–1 Reading Interest Survey

Reading Interest Survey

1. What is your favorite TV program?
2. Who are your favorite TV characters?
3. Check all of your interests
   - ❏ humorous situations
   - ❏ fairy tales
   - ❏ adventure stories
   - ❏ family stories
   - ❏ science fiction
   - ❏ mysteries
   - ❏ current events
   - ❏ nature/animals
   - ❏ science
   - ❏ cartoons
   - ❏ sports
   - ❏ music
   - ❏ real people
   - ❏ fantasy
   - ❏ poetry
   - ❏ informational stories
   - ❏ history
   - ❏ Other _____
4. Who are your favorite sports stars? _____
5. Who are your favorite musicians?_____
6. What is your favorite hobby?_____
7. What is your favorite pet? _____
8. What is your favorite book? _____
9. Who is your favorite author? _____
10. What is your favorite activity outside of school? _____
11. What things do you like to collect? _____
12. What are your favorite subjects in school? _____
13. Name some place you would like to visit. _____
14. What do you like best about the public library? _____
15. What topics would you like to know more about? _____
16. Do you belong to any clubs or groups? _____
17. Name some books you have read recently. _____

Knowing the student is more complex. Think about each student's psychological, social, and intellectual development, reading level, interest level, learning style, and personal interests. Find out what he has read and enjoyed in the past. Your task then becomes matching the right book or nonprint item to the individual student. He might say he has read nothing he enjoyed, so have a few surefire hits for both boys and girls. Your challenge is to guide the student to the next skill level and help him develop lifelong learning skills. Encourage variety in reading and viewing materials and introduce new items. Try to find out what students think of an item when they return it.

Hone your readers' advisory skills. Try to have regular book discussions with teachers, other librarians, and those students who are readers. Use book vendors' Web sites and read those promotional materials. Some Web sites devoted to reader's advisory are Book Browser (*www.bookbrowser.com*), Overbooked (*www.overbooked.com*), and Reader's Robot (*tnrdlib.bc.ca/rr.html*). Subscription services are available such as NoveList (*novelist.epnet.com/login.html*), part of the EBSCO services. The reading interest survey in Figure 9–1 is also a useful tool.

TEACHING INFORMATION SKILLS

The library media center is at the heart of the curriculum. Proficiency in information skills facilitates learning in all subject areas. The library media specialist is the school's expert in this area and therefore needs to provide appropriate instruction. Do not try to teach library skills in isolation; bibliographic instruction is more effective when the skills are taught as part of a teaching unit. This means involvement with the teacher at the planning stages of a unit and input into the curriculum. An isolated exercise on using a particular database is not as effective as using that database to find articles for a report or class research project such as on a popular rock star. A student will remember how to use a resource when she gets results on a particular activity.

The 1998 edition of *Information Power* outlines nine standards for information literacy. Student achievement is at the heart of these guidelines. This has become the action plan for the mission put down in the earlier version in 1988.

The Nine Information Literacy Standards
for Student Learning

Information Literacy
Standard 1: The student who is information literate accesses information efficiently and effectively.
Standard 2: The student who is information literate evaluates information critically and competently.
Standard 3: The student who is information literate uses information accurately and creatively.

Independent Learning
Standard 4: The student who is an independent learner is information literate and pursues information related to personal interests.
Standard 5: The student who is an independent learner is information literate and appreciates literature and other creative expressions of information.
Standard 6: The student who is an independent learner is information literate and strives for excellence in information seeking and knowledge generation.
Social Responsibility
Standard 7: The student who contributes positively to the learning community and to society is information literate and recognizes the importance of information to a democratic society.
Standard 8: The student who contributes positively to the learning community and to society is information literate and practices ethical behavior in regard to information and information technology.
Standard 9: The student who contributes positively to the learning community and to society is information literate and participates effectively in groups to pursue and generate information (ALA, 1998: 8–9).

The standards are used in tandem with any curriculum. In order to merge the two goals, you and the teacher plan the lesson together. Emphasize that this will not make more work for the teacher. His job will actually be easier because you are sharing it with him. Use a good collaboration form to help facilitate the process (see Figure 9–2).

HOW DO YOU GET INVOLVED WITH CURRICULUM?

Curriculum planning? Consider:
- materials
- content: facts, ideas, concepts, skills, attitudes
- activities

If you are to be part of the overall educational program, you need to understand curriculum and find ways to motivate teachers to use the media center. Attend all faculty and departmental meetings and contribute. If your schedule will not allow you to attend them all, attend at least one meeting of each department and request minutes from the other meetings. Become thoroughly familiar with the teaching methods being used (e.g., team teaching, whole language approach, and so on).

Figure 9–2 Collaborative Planning Worksheet

DATE: _____/_____/_____

COLLABORATIVE PLANNING SHEET
Carrollton-Farmers Branch I.S.D.

Teacher:
Library Media Specialist:
Campus:
Content Area:
GOALS AND OBJECTIVES:

PROPOSED LEARNING ACTIVITIES:

EXPECTATIONS FOR CLASSROOM TEACHER:

EXPECTATIONS FOR LIBRARY MEDIA SPECIALIST:

EXPECTATIONS FOR THE STUDENTS:

STUDENT OUTCOME OR EVALUATION:

**TEACHER/LIBRARY MEDIA SPECIALIST EVALUATION OF A
COLLABORATIVE LESSON (to be filled in with the teacher)**

L.M.S.:   Campus:
Unit Title:
What worked well in the unit?
Suggestions for improvement:
How well did the library media center collection support the lesson objectives?
  5 = excellent; 4 = above average; 3 = average; 2 = below average; 1 = poor
            variety of media (print and nonprint)
            materials are current (as required by the topic)
            materials are relevant
            materials are in acceptable condition
            enough material was available for the number of students
            materials span reading/viewing/listening levels of students
            materials span opinion/cultural/political issues
            materials appeal to student interests

AVERAGE OF THE ABOVE RATINGS

5.00–4.5 = exemplary; 4.49–3.75 = recognized; 3.74–3 = acceptable; below 3 = not acceptable

---

Figure 9–2 *Continued*

The initial purpose of page one is to help the LMS and the classroom teacher collaborate to deter- mine and articulate what each will do with students when they are in the LMC and what the end product will be. The goal is to maximize students' time by creating clear objectives and direction for their library experience.

Once the lesson or activity is over, it is critical that the LMS go back to the teacher and the class to determine how adequate the resources were that were available in the LMC. This is often the step missing in a library lesson. While many librarians and authors encourage teacher input, collec- tion development is often driven by intuition, random recommendations, or a long-range plan devel- oped by the librarian. Page two of this form provides data that can be used in a number of ways.

- The collaboration form provides documentation for the LMS and the classroom teacher for col- laboration outside their department, which is an important part of the state's (and district's) pro- fessional evaluation form; often classroom teachers have come back to the LMS to ask for cop- ies to include in a portfolio or documentation folder.

- The feedback provided on the form gives the librarian documentation on which parts of the active collection are most in need of weeding or further development during the current or following year. The numerical scoring helps to provide a basis for materials selection when financial resources are limited: with a stack of substandard evaluations, a part of the collection receiving "1" is more critical than a "2" would be. This process is both program/resource evaluation and collection development.

- The feedback provided on the evaluation form is shared with the director (each campus submits a minimum of one evaluation per week. The director formulates budgets based on the "Texas Standards for School Library Media Centers" (1997) and includes additional requests for funds based on the documentation submitted by the campus. While everyone can always use more budget, having a weighted scale for needs provides direction for the coming year.

This work sheet is based on work by David V. Loertscher from his book, *Taxonomies of the School Library Media Program* (2000), with his permission

---

Become involved with curriculum committees in your school and district. A great deal of "new" curriculum includes informa- tion skills. Find out about and participate in curriculum at the earliest planning stage. Point out the information skills and emphasize to your faculty that you can help them achieve the goals set forth in their curriculum. Order materials that match subjects and grade and ability levels. Add subject headings from the curriculum to the catalog and the vertical file. Get feedback from teachers on materials and let them preview before purchas- ing. Use your knowledge of learning styles to choose varied media for instructional units.

You might be able to participate in curriculum development at the district and state levels. Become aware and supportive of your colleagues who are politically savvy at this level and you will find a way to become involved or at least informed. These factors will help you form and realize your own instructional vision for curriculum development at your school.

Because of your special knowledge of educational resources, you can recommend resources in the media center that are helpful. In addition, you might be able to make your own resources by adapting materials from other sources to use in a unit.

Develop and produce audiovisual materials as needed for instructional units. This can include making off-air videotapes, slides and audiotapes, overhead transparencies, and so on. Be sure you know current copyright laws before producing copies. Post a copy of the current law in your media center so if or when you are asked to produce an item in violation of copyright law, you can explain why you cannot fulfill the request.

Check whether your district has an agreement with the local educational station or other sources for reproduction rights. Secure equipment, materials, and services from this source to use in instructional units.

Information Power (pages 4–5) suggests the following guidelines for involvement as an instructional consultant:

> As instructional partner, the library media specialist joins with teachers and others to identify links across student information needs, curricular content, learning outcomes, and a wide variety of print, nonprint, and electronic information resources. Working with the entire school community, the library media specialist takes a leading role in developing policies, practices, and curricula that guide students to develop the full range of information and communication abilities. Committed to the process of collaboration, the library media specialist works closely with individual teachers in the critical areas of designing the authentic learning tasks and assessments and integrating the information and communication abilities required to meet subject matter standards.

ORIENTATION

This is one lesson that can be separate from the curriculum, but if there is a way to include a curriculum item in the orientation, it is more effective. It is desirable and necessary to make contact with students and faculty and introduce them to the media center and your policies early in the year. Although an orientation for all students would be repetitious for some, everyone needs a little reminder of the media center's procedures. If classes are on a fixed library schedule, make the orientation part of each class's first visit. Work with all teachers of subjects such as English and social studies, even science, so all students visit the library.

Make a schedule for new teacher and student orientations. Then remind teachers in advance with a written notice. Invite your principal and returning teachers. You might want to include a notice in your library newsletter (if you have one) or other school publication.

Keep your presentation brief, friendly, and positive. Introduce your staff. State your policies, including when and how students can use the media center and check out books, how you handle overdue and lost materials, and if interlibrary loans are available. This is also the right time to promote your special activities or clubs.

Handouts are helpful and can include:

- floor plan of the media center
- brochure of services
- bibliography of new books and materials
- list of magazines and newspapers
- bibliography of the professional collection for teachers

Provide additional information for new teachers, such as procedures for check out of equipment and other materials, scheduling of classes, and any other special services offered.

Many media specialists prepare a slide/tape, video, or PowerPoint orientation to their media center. This is most helpful when orientation is to be repeated and it can be used on an individual basis for late-enrolling students.

AFTER ORIENTATION, WILL YOU TEACH AGAIN?

Selling the concept of integrating skills into the curriculum now takes on a daily priority. Convince administrators of the importance of information literacy in every student's education. In turn, have the administrators encourage teachers to incorporate information skills units in their plans and to plan this with you. If information skills activities are not part of the subject area curriculum, work with subject teachers to include them. The fact that many standardized tests include information gathering and usage justifies the need for these skills to be part of the curriculum.

You know that you should be a partner, but do other teachers know they should be a partner with you? Evaluate your program so your lessons are effective and current. Have an arsenal of lessons, ideas, and activities that can be incorporated into the teachers' plans, keeping the idea alive that you and the teachers are a team working together for the students' benefit. Initiate planning sessions with confidence because you have valuable contributions to make. Determine a teacher's need and make specific suggestions rather than vague offers of help. Find out when the teacher's planning time is and go to meet with her.

The typical planning process includes these factors: Preliminary needs assessment has helped you understand your student group, their information needs, preferred learning styles, interests, and knowledge level. You have identified your skill objective based on the curriculum. You are ready to go to your lesson plan.

LESSON PLANNING:
- Teacher knows:
  students
  content area
- Library media specialist knows:
  resources
  information skills

- *Objective*: State specifically what the learning involves so the outcome is specified.
- *Content*: Provide information. Will you present new information or are you reviewing?
- *Methodology*: Provide examples, models, illustrations relevant to the students' backgrounds and learning styles.
- *Checking for understanding*: Know ahead of time how you will check the things you want the students to be able to do.
- *Activities*: Allow students to practice with your guidance.
- *Independent practice*: Allow students to practice on their own.
- *Evaluation*: A must so you will know if you succeeded. You also will be able to measure the students' mastery of the objectives.

You might want to use your school's printed form for lesson plans to guide you. Depending on your level of involvement with other teachers, this could entail a single unit or a sequential program of lessons. Your goal is to move from being involved only in the activities phase to being an active partner in the other phases, particularly planning the objectives. A variety of teaching aids are also available through educational or library supply sources.

These include workbooks, filmstrips, transparencies, videos, and bulletin board materials. See Appendix H for a list of suppliers of instructional aids and Appendix C for audiovisual producers.

Since the teacher will naturally have more understanding of the individual students, you can benefit very much from finding out all you can about your students. This can be accomplished by distributing interest surveys, giving pretests, observing students in the media center, conferring with their teachers, and discovering preferred learning styles. It is important to develop a collection of materials that address all students' styles and, when teaching, to accommodate student differences.

HOW DO YOU FIND OUT ABOUT INDIVIDUAL STUDENT STYLES?

There are many learning style inventories available for use with students in the media center. These range from simple paper/pencil tests or observation techniques to computerized tests and scoring. Appendix M contains a sample test you might choose to try, provided by John W. Pelley from Texas Tech University. It is based on the Myers-Briggs Type Indicator for personality types. Pelley has developed a questionnaire based on this system to determine learning styles.

By going to the Web site, the student responds to a series of questions, picking which one of opposite statements best describes his comfort in working one way or another. Scoring is simple. The student will receive a four-letter code that indicates aspects of his learning style. Then he can click on a link that will describe the characteristics of the learning type.

With this information, lessons can be developed to accommodate students' preferred styles and can also be designed to strengthen weaker modes. If you have assessed your students' needs and know what should be taught and how to approach your students, you can develop your own curriculum. Many school districts have a standard library/media center curriculum in place. Your needs assessment might make it necessary, however, to supplement your standard curriculum.

HOW DO THE STUDENTS PLAN THEIR RESEARCH?

You will find many good methods for teaching the lessons that you develop with your teachers. Big 6, I-Search, Flip-it, and other methods can provide you with excellent models for lessons. All of these methods emphasize the need to teach the student to plan her search strategy. This involves a planning stage on the student's part before she ever begins her research. Graphic organizers can help with the planning phase as students work on their search strategy. Here are some valuable steps at the heart of these organizational methods:

1. What information do I need? Background information, point of view, specific information? Have the students know what they are looking for.
2. Where will I look? Familiarize the students with available databases, then have them list the databases that could help them.
3. What keywords will I use? Brainstorm keywords and analyze the possible success/failure ahead of time.
4. What is the difference between subject and keyword? Which would be better for the type of information the students need?
5. How do I need to modify my search? After some trial and error, how can the students change their search strategy for more success?
6. What worked and what didn't? After the initial research, take time to evaluate.

HOW DO STUDENTS EVALUATE INFORMATION?

Another key component in many of the research methods is evaluation of the material that is found during research. The student must learn to judge whether the information is relevant to his information needs based on the planning he did as demonstrated above, as well as evaluate whether the information itself is accurate. If the information is in a book, then it has at least gone through an editing process. However, information in the media or on the Internet might not have gone through this rigorous process. Evaluation of information then becomes a very important step as students get information from more and more sources.

Television and other media sources require critical thinking skills that frequently go unaddressed. This "media literacy" has some unique aspects that the library media specialist is in an ideal position to incorporate into her lessons.

1. *Access*: Cable and other technologies are part of the library/ media center and are often broadcast throughout the building through the library.
2. *Analysis*: Critical thinking skills that the library/media specialist teaches can be applied to the media messages received through television.
3. *Evaluation*: Modeling opportunities are available to the library/media specialist to evaluate, compare, and contrast the value of media messages.

CLUES OF MISINFOR-MATION:
- requests for money
- contradictions
- errors: spelling, grammar, mathematical
- emotional messages: fear, guilt, flattery
- opinion words: "I think"
- illogical arguments
- obvious bias
- "Pass this message on"
- no author credentials

4. *Production*: The library is an ideal location for students to apply their insights into productions of their own.

The area of most recent concern involves the evaluation of information received on the Internet. The ease of publishing on the Internet has increased the chance of misinformation, conflicting information, and even malicious information. Knowing the origins of the information helps to identify the problems.

1. *Always be critical*. Be alert for the clues to misinformation.
2. *Build a knowledge base*. Before going to the Internet, have a working knowledge of the information you are seeking.
3. *Know the difference between fact and opinion*. Practice recognizing fact from opinion before going on the Internet.
4. *Look for logical arguments*. Be alert for arguments that are backed up with facts not simply oversimplification or pat answers.
5. *Compare information against other sources*. This strategy is always a good tool for verifying information.
6. *Look for authority of source*. Look for evidence that the author of the Web site has expertise.
7. *Look for bias*. Political agendas and commercials can be subtle.
8. *Guard against assumptions*. Just because it is on the computer does not make it true.

Make sure students know when the material is from a database of magazine, journal, or newspaper articles. While the articles have been through the editing process to make it into print, students should still verify the information in other sources.

USING A RESEARCH METHOD SUCH AS I-SEARCH

One method that is particularly successful for research projects is the I-search writing process, originally developed by Ken Macrorie and adapted for the school library media specialist by Marilyn Joyce and Julie Tallman in *Making the Writing and Research Connection with the I-Search Process* (Neal-Schuman, 1997). These ideas are elaborated further by Donna Duncan and Laura Lockhart in *I-Search, You Search, We All Learn to Research* (Neal-Schuman, 2000). When using this method, be sure to allow plenty of time for the process to unfold, as this method can take longer than traditional research projects because of the need for frequent conferencing with the student. Tallman's extensive research on this shows that students do make the transfer of these skills to their next assignments, making the process quicker, easier, and more meaningful for them in subsequent research.

Steps to this process are four basic strategies:

> **Step 1:** Build background knowledge on a theme. Students are not only introduced to new material, but they explore what they already know about the theme. At the end of this phase, the student picks a topic and formulates a statement that is interesting to him.
>
> **Step 2:** Students now formulate their search strategy for how they will gather information: print sources, audiovisual sources, personal interviews, or experimenting.
>
> **Step 3:** Next, begin actual information gathering and analyzing and assimilating the knowledge.
>
> **Step 4:** Students write, edit, and publish their final product, as well as report what they learned from the research process.

A valuable aspect to this method is allowing the students to reflect on their progress at each step of the process. Starting a journal at the beginning of the research is the recommended way to fulfill this need. The students are given time to reflect on what they are interested in to begin with, what they felt about the information they found along the way, and how it answered their questions. This can be incorporated into the final product.

The journal can also be a way for students to verbalize what they already know about the topic they have chosen. A three-column form is helpful in making them organize what they know, what they do not know, and what they want to know. This step is not for detailed note taking. They are urged to reflect on the information they have found and record general impressions.

Now the students are ready to examine more sources. The more information they gather, the more a form or outline should become obvious. If students cannot see an organizational pattern emerging, they might need more information. Journal writing can help students evaluate the information they found, aiding them to find solutions themselves to the problems they encountered. Students are urged to compare material found from different sources.

Journal writing helps students make the transition to their final product. They can use portions of their journal as their rough draft, easing into the report writing. The final step of self-assessment comes directly from the journal reflection and then becomes part of the report. Teacher comments written in journals can be guiding tools rather than an arbitrary grade.

This method is a direct result of a classroom teacher and a teacher-librarian working together, utilizing the strengths of both professionals in the research process. Use this example as a way of collaborating to foster real learning and encouraging your teaching staff to work with you. Because the media center is an extension of the classroom, you have a unique opportunity to present material in creative and exciting ways.

10 PROGRAMMING

TIP: Maintain a file of community resources. Have information on all libraries in your area: public, academic, and special. Also, get acquainted with community and government agencies, businesses, and public utilities. Keep a speaker file of people with special skills and interests, especially local writers.

The special programs you plan are sure to attract the entire school's attention. Special programs provide a break from the routine of everyday school life and can provide some of the most memorable school experiences for you, the teachers, and the students.

Special programs include promotional programs, reading contests, speakers, storytellers, book fairs, Reading Is Fundamental (RIF) distributions, visiting authors, puppet shows, and media presentations. Library media specialists do many creative programs for such special activities. Individual events featuring reading periods involving everybody in the school—sometimes called D.E.A.R. for Drop Everything and Read—are popular and widespread.

YOU AS A STORYTELLER

Some people think storytelling is a spontaneous event between the storyteller and an audience, but it is really an art form. As with any art form, there are skill levels that can be improved by practicing.

The storyteller shares in the oldest known educational tradition. Storytelling is not memorizing a story and repeating it word for word. Although memorization is helpful, a storyteller learns how to tell a story in tune with the audience. The idea of relating a story with few or no props or books is intimidating, but more direct contact is possible between the storyteller and the audience when such items are kept to a minimum.

If you want to learn a story to tell, begin with something short and relatively simple. Never tell a story you do not like. If you do, you will spend a lot of time working on a story that simply will not work for you. Put the main events on note cards. Memorize any phrases or details that are vital to the story. Read the story in its printed form several times, both silently and aloud. Practice the story. Try practicing in front of a mirror, then on a pet, and then on your family. If you need to make changes, jot some notes on your main event cards. The first time you tell a story, use your cards and you will not be as nervous.

Watch other practiced storytellers. Each one has his own style, and you will develop your own. You should have a beginning to your story, which may or may not be "Once upon a time . . . ."

Some storytellers use a candle; as long as the candle burns, no one talks except the storyteller. You probably have some classroom control technique that will serve as an opening. By the same token, each story should have an ending. "Well, that's all" is a letdown to the story experience.

You will want to put inflection into your voice as you tell your story. Be careful with dialects. Unless you are very familiar with a dialect, do not try to use it. However, the way you phrase your sentences can give a dialectical lilt to the story without your resorting to the dialect itself. Keep your gestures simple and fluid.

As you become more proficient, you can add props, games, pictures, even music to your stories.

FLANNEL BOARD

One way to bridge story reading and storytelling is to use a flannel board. By manipulating your flannel characters, you will put main events into action. You can put reminders on the characters themselves.

Flannel boards can be purchased from educational suppliers, or you can make your own with cardboard or wood. If you make your own, cover it with a dark-colored, fuzzy material. You can make your figures from Pellon®, a commercially made interfacing available at fabric stores. Trace the pattern on the Pellon, outline with a black felt-tip pen, and color with markers, crayons, or whatever you like best. To make background pieces from felt for extra color, make a photocopy of your pattern, cut it out, and trace around it.

Learn stories for the flannel board in the same way as for storytelling. Be sure to practice the story with the board and the pieces before you tell the story to an audience.

PUPPETRY

You do not have to be a professional puppeteer to bring new excitement to your library time with puppets. Children love puppets in a special way. They love to watch them, and they love to make them talk. Puppets give children a way to communicate emotions that are otherwise difficult to put into words. For example, show a puppet having a temper tantrum and help the puppet find a way to channel his temper. Perhaps the child who watches can later visualize the solution when she begins to throw a temper tantrum.

When using puppets, the most important thing to remember is the puppet's character. When you get a puppet, name it, make it a "him" or a "her." Decide if it will be smart or slow, talk high or low. Then do not change the character of the puppet. You might want to use the same puppet in more than one story. If the character you have established for the puppet is not appropriate for the story, disguise it. Nothing is more distracting than for a seven-year-old to exclaim in horror, "But that's not Harry the Dirty Dog! That's Scruffy!"

You can use puppets easily—you do not need a fancy puppet theater. Try talking to the puppet. The puppet might be too shy to talk and hide its face in your shoulder. There could be a character who forgets how to count when playing hide and seek. Or, you could tell a story with your puppet. Learn your story as if you were storytelling. If you are worried about forgetting the story, open the book or lay out your notes so you can refer to them easily. The children will not be bothered by your notes, your exposed arm, or your mouth moving; they will be fascinated by the puppet and willing to believe the puppet's character as soon as you give it life.

You could begin with a commercially made puppet, but you will have to use someone else's concept of the puppet's character. Once you get used to using puppets, you will not always be able to find a ready-made puppet that embodies the character you want. Then your creativity will run wild. Puppets can be made from socks, felt, soft sculpture, paper sacks, paper plates, anything else you can imagine. Even a cardboard figure on a spoon can be considered a puppet.

As your puppet productions become more elaborate, try new things. Record the dialogue, sound effects, or music and let someone else operate the puppets. If time allows, let the children make simple puppets. Older children can perform more complex puppet plays for their classmates or younger students. This will require coordination from you and dedicated rehearsing from the students, but it is good fun.

Dos and Don'ts for Booktalking

DO:
• Make notes
• Hook the listener
• Practice
• Say title and author first and last
• Point cover of book at listeners

DON'T:
• Tell the ending
• Talk about a book you haven't read

BOOKTALKS

This classroom-extending activity is meant to create an atmosphere of enriching literature. Booktalks are a little storytelling and a little advertisement. If you feel you do not have time for or are simply intimidated by booktalking, you are not alone. Think of booktalking as sharing your enthusiasm for books. Once you start a booktalk, that enthusiasm is contagious and the students' excitement will feed yours.

Always remember that you are trying to sell the book, so never tell the ending. If you do, the student has no need to read the book. Always talk about a work that you have read. It is too easy to get flustered and stammer when you are asked questions about a book you have not read.

When preparing a booktalk (and preparation is the most important step), read a lot so you will have plenty to choose from. It is easier to remember things about the book if you write down details to jog your memory, such as title, author, brief plot, important characters, exciting or unusual incidents from the book, and page numbers. Always start with an attention getter that will entice your reader to try the book. Practice and time your booktalk. Say the title and author first and last in your talk. Have something visual to go with your talk. If the book has an appealing dust jacket, you could use that. If you are using an old or unattractive copy of the book, use something more attractive as your visual hook.

After you have done some formal booktalks, your informal ones will become easier and more effective. Booktalking of all kinds will not only boost your library's circulation, it will encourage students to read—one of the most rewarding parts of your job. Establish a program of booktalking. Avid and reluctant readers alike will want to get a book and find out what happens.

COMPILING BIBLIOGRAPHIES

Bibliographies are useful tools to direct students and teachers to frequently used subjects. You can create subject bibliographies for a particular unit of study or make promotional bibliographies of fiction or new books. The Children's Book Council and the American Library Association have bibliographies that you can use and adapt for your purposes. Look at their Web sites at *www.cbcbooks.org*, *www.ala.org/alsc*, and *www.ala.org/yalsa* to get ideas. Most states have a reading promotion from their state library association with a bibliography and promotional materials.

When a teacher makes an assignment and all the students are asking for books on that subject, you can provide better guidance to everyone with a bibliography. Students also benefit from a bibliography compiled strictly for pleasure reading. Once you have compiled a bibliography, it can be used over again in subsequent years and new materials can be added easily.

Here are steps for compiling a bibliography:

1. Choose your subject, look up the subject in the catalog, and decide which titles to use. You might limit your titles to an appropriate grade or reading level or use some other criterion. Check professional tools that give bibliographic data; you might find subject headings you did not try previously.
2. Decide whether or not to include annotations. Many bibliographies do not need them, and annotating will slow you down.
3. Type the bibliography, including the call numbers.
4. Make copies and put them in one place. This could be somewhere at the circulation desk, in a file cabinet, or in a sorter where students can reach them easily.
5. Keep a copy on file. Date the bibliography so you will know when to update it. As you process books, add new titles on the appropriate bibliography to simplify the updating.

SERVICES TO TEACHERS

HOW CAN YOU ENHANCE COMMUNICATION WITH TEACHERS?

To achieve an instructional team spirit, try some outreach activities to let faculty and administration know you are eager to work with them. Get acquainted with teachers and administrators and know them as individuals. Join them in the teachers' lounge and eat lunch with them. Many ideas are tried out in this informal atmosphere. Work with teachers to develop units of study and include library skills instruction. Also, visit classes or initiate a booktalk program.

Produce newsletters, either print or electronic, and include lists of new materials and highlight special events or collections. You could produce a flyer with seasonal information from sources in the library, saying, "All this information is in your media center."

Distribute bibliographies for upcoming special events, for example, books featured for Black History Month, holidays, and special school projects.

Provide a quiet escape for teachers in the media center with coffee, reading materials, and soft furniture, if possible. Try a paperback exchange of bestsellers in your teachers' area.

CONDUCTING AN IN-SERVICE PROGRAM FOR FACULTY AND STAFF

The steps for planning an in-service program for teachers are similar to those for teaching students, but teachers have special needs that make the planning and pretesting stage especially important. First, be sure to involve teachers in the planning of the program. Other suggested steps include:

1. pretesting
2. statement of objectives
3. planning of activities
4. evaluation

Conduct a survey to determine what teachers need and want to know; list in-service options and ask teachers for their opinions. Write a statement that specifies an outcome. Specific objectives are very important for in-service. Determine what activities will accomplish the stated objectives. Small groups might work better than large ones. Provide opportunities for practice and for evaluation of mastery of the objectives. A series of in-service opportunities that build sequentially on each other is often popular. Ask again for opinions to help you plan the next program. Be available for follow-up needs after in-service.

Motivational incentives for teachers include release time from class, staff development credit, or advanced training credit.

WHAT ABOUT HAVING CONTESTS?

Set your requirements and offer prizes. Reading contests are based on how much a student reads. Some contests are run according to the number of books read; some give prizes according to the amount of time spent reading. A parent or other adult will verify whether the student fulfilled the requirements.

Older students enjoy research-type contests such as "find the answer" or trivia contests. You might want to require the source and page number where the student found the answer as verification.

Make sure the prizes are worthwhile. Find out what is valuable to students. See if merchants or community businesses will donate prizes for you to use. Fast-food coupons or movie passes are popular prizes. If you receive a gift with an order, such as a clock or a camera, you could use that for a contest prize. If your school has a corporate sponsor, the sponsor could supply prizes. If you must spend money for prizes, you will find that buying in bulk will supply you with prizes for several contests but that students might lose interest if they get the same thing over and over again. Overdue fines can be a source for money to buy prizes.

SHOULD YOU HAVE A BOOK FAIR?

There are many positive reasons for having a book fair, but there is a lot of work involved. Be prepared!

Pride of owning books contributes to a student's love of reading. A book fair is one way to help a student develop a personal library. You have a chance to "talk books" with students and aid them in their own book selection. In addition, if you run the book fair, you will be able to use the profits to build your program. If you have a book fair during the Christmas season, you can have the satisfaction of knowing that family members and students will be receiving books as gifts.

In choosing a company, consider the amount of profit you will keep, if promotional materials are provided, and how the company handles orders if you run out of popular titles.

Once the decision is made to have a book fair and you have chosen the company, begin to plan at once. Advertising is essential, and you will need time to put the event on the school calendar, put ads in the school paper and in the various school announcements, send letters home to parents, and talk to teachers. Scheduling is another factor. Teachers appreciate being included in the planning of events. You might want to schedule a book fair during Open House.

Recruit help from volunteers and school personnel. Give them a schedule and a brief description of how the fair will operate. Plan a reward for them.

You will need to have these things on hand:

- receipt book or calculator that prints receipts
- coin wrappers
- money box (preferably one that locks)
- change
- request forms (in case someone wants a book that is sold out)
- pens

When the books arrive, group similar books together, such as mysteries, award winners, science fiction, nonfiction, and so on. Devise a system to signal when titles are sold out. Label the last book so that it will not be sold and the students will know they can order a copy of this popular title. The book fair company will help you with planning materials and checklists.

WHAT IS RIF?

Reading Is Fundamental (RIF) is a federally sponsored program that provides money for books so children who might not have books in their homes can own some.

RIF distributions are similar to book fairs without the worry of collecting money. Many book fair companies or paperback book suppliers make ordering for RIF easy. You can order sets or individual titles.

When you are ready for distribution, arrange the books in attractive ways and allow students to choose. Devise a form that can give you a count for statistics. Students can write in the names of the books they choose so you will know which books are popular enough for future ordering.

HOW DO YOU ARRANGE FOR A SPEAKER?

One of the most exciting things you can do is bring in a speaker that the students enjoy. Your challenge is to find a speaker who has something meaningful to say and can relate to your students. If you tie in a speaker with a lesson unit, your search will have some focus.

Create and maintain a speaker file. Youth librarians from the public library will often do booktalks for your students. Storyteller and writer groups have members who are interested in performing and speaking. Business persons can be a source for career talks. Local celebrities might volunteer. Network with other library media specialists for names of successful speakers at their schools.

You must limit the audience in some way. You could reward

reading contest winners with attendance at the speaker's event or invite classes who are studying the speaker's area of expertise. Once you know who will attend, schedule the classes. A written reminder is helpful to teachers. If the classes do not arrive within five or ten minutes of the scheduled time, send someone to remind the teacher. If possible, videotape the event.

If you need to rearrange the furniture in the media center, give yourself plenty of time to move things around. Have the camera or cameras ready. After the event, allow yourself time to readjust to your normal schedule. If you are paying your speaker, have the check ready that day. If you are not paying, a gift is appropriate. (A school memento is nice.) If nothing else, write a thank-you note or encourage students to write to the speaker.

Countdown to Visiting Author
- One Year to Six Months: contract the author.
- Six Weeks: Order books.
- Four Weeks: Read and promote books to students.
- Three Weeks: Communicate with parents.
- Two Weeks: Sponsor art and story competitions with winners receiving autographed copies of the books.
- That Day: Make it a media day; generate lots of sales.

WHAT ABOUT A VISITING AUTHOR?

Visiting authors create very special events. If possible, do not limit your audience. In this case, the event cannot take place in the media center, and your planning must be on a larger scale.

Publishers are a valuable resource in planning an author visit, but have several authors or illustrators in mind when you call them. You will want to have an author who is appropriate for your school and one who appeals to your students, so there should be a common thread among the names on your list. Plan with your principal so you know when you want the author to come, but have more than one date so you can be responsive to his schedule. Plan with bookstores and the public library so you know what you want the author to do and where else in the community the author will visit while in town. Your district might be able to help you get a well-known author, or several media specialists can get together and plan visits for the author's trip. The author could charge a flat fee or a fee plus lodging and transportation. You might need to pick the author up at the airport.

For the day of the event, make sure the auditorium or the cafeteria is set up in plenty of time with any audiovisual equipment or microphones needed by the author. If possible, plan to sell or take orders for books so students can get autographed copies. Autographing can take place in the library or at a reception in the lounge. Take lots of pictures!

The publisher or the author can provide posters and publicity materials. Be sure to advertise to parents when there are book sales involved. Parents might be interested in helping with various arrangements and also buy books as gifts.

Once the author has left, be sure to thank everyone. Write a thank-you note to the author and include photographs, if possible. A note or group project from the students is always appreciated. Continue the celebration by displaying photographs after the event and continue to read the author's books and plan activities around remarks made by the author.

Evaluate the program. Get feedback from teachers and students. Be sure to record your list of things you wish you had done differently. Publishers also appreciate feedback after an author visit so they can make their program more effective. For a complete guide to author visits, consult Kathy East's *Inviting Children's Authors and Illustrators: A How-To-Do-It Manual for School and Public Librarians* (Neal-Schuman, 1995).

PROMOTING THE MEDIA CENTER

WHY PROMOTE THE MEDIA CENTER?

Think of your program as a product. You work hard to make your product good. Now you need to present your product to your consumers. Marketing is ongoing; almost everything you do creates an image of the library. If you have satisfied customers—students, teachers, and administrators—they will come back and recommend you to their friends and colleagues. Think about your own image. A smile and an attitude of enthusiasm create a positive image. Be receptive to suggestions. Select a theme for the year that could make the media center the center of attention in the school. You might want to use the National Library Week-ALA theme of the year, or you can choose your own. If you have a library club, those students can help develop the theme and make plans to carry it out.

WHAT ACTIVITIES PROMOTE THE MEDIA CENTER?

Variety is a key to promotion. Try new things all the time, but constantly remind the school about the media center. Place short, funny, positive notices about the library media center in school announcements.

Submit articles to the school newspaper or have a student reporter do a regular column on media center activities. News items could include new materials, trivia items, unusual happenings, interesting services. Newsletters appeal to teachers, staff, and administration.

Create displays and exhibits. Print a brochure of student services. Choose a theme. Have a student contest to submit themes. Bookmarks and pencils are popular as prizes. Give away posters to teachers who enjoy "freebies." If you have a production workshop, allow students and teachers to keep their products.

Contests can be a good way to highlight new services that are not being heavily used. You might not feel the need to promote programs that are already being used, but remember that "nothing succeeds like success." Promotion can make them used even better. Have students make tapes of their own book reviews of new materials. Many students like to read or hear what others have enjoyed.

Present new materials during faculty meetings. Invite faculty for teas in the media center to introduce new materials or services. Invite groups to use the library as a meeting place. Become involved with the PTA. Members can help you with special activities and elicit volunteer help.

WHAT MAKES A DISPLAY EFFECTIVE?

Use displays in promoting your media center. Use the bulletin board or other display areas to teach and to support curriculum, as well as to tell about the library. Dramatize the media center as a key part of the school's instructional program, of value to the lifelong learning needs of every student.

If your displays do not attract attention, part of your message is lost. Bulletin board supplies are available from a variety of sources such as library suppliers or through educational supply catalogs (see Appendix D).

Be sure to change your displays often. Make them visually attractive. Use colors, different textures, and three-dimensional items for variety. Present information clearly. Make letters large and easy to read from a distance.

Focus the subject of a display. Use one central concept. Keep the display simple and uncluttered. Be clever, even humorous, with captions.

Involve students. Design displays around the students' interests: class work, candid photos, school sports and events. Encourage students to offer their ideas.

TO WEB OR NOT TO WEB

More and more librarians are turning to a Web page to promote their library and library services. It is a valuable source of information for your patrons, so by all means consider it. A good Web page can also help you organize the services you offer, especially electronic ones, and help your patrons use them more effectively. In essence, you can create a self-paced electronic classroom.

Web Pages: Do Your Homework
- Have a working knowledge of the technology.
- Learn graphic design basics.
- Plan to frequently update.
- Be creative.

If you are not technologically gifted, you can recruit help from others who are: teachers, parents, and students can all help you mount the kind of Web page you will be proud to show. Familiarize yourself with the elements of a good Web page before you start.

The basics of Web design are straightforward enough. Depending on your level of involvement with the page itself, a working knowledge of the technology needed to mount your Web page is valuable. Be familiar with what graphic design elements work and those that do not, i.e., too busy, too distracting, and so on. Have a plan in place to update the page regularly. A current Web page is essential to its success. You have a chance to show your creative side by making an organized, useful, and attractive page that users find helpful.

Using the basics of Web page design, librarians have been able to tie library activities to curriculum projects and individualize instruction for classes. Other librarians have linked subscription services to a Web page. Your page then becomes a vehicle to deliver specialized services according to your goals. Keep your Web page flexible as your goals change or expand.

Here are some general guidelines to keep in mind as you design your Web page:

- Planning is essential: Consider what you want to convey with the Web page, who are your patrons, how is the information organized, and how does this site look.
- Let the information be your guide: Design around the information goals you have for the page.
- Be consistent: Move from page to page in the same way.
- Be logical: Move from general to specific in rational steps.
- Be aware of how your page will work on all browsers and all kinds of equipment. Consider how quickly your page loads. If someone is using a slower modem, she may become impatient with the time your page loads. This might affect your decision to include video or audio.
- Be sure users can navigate through your site easily. Use buttons, especially back buttons to the main page.
- Get feedback from your users to find what works and does not work. Incorporate suggestions as they fit your goals.
- Be aware of changing technology so you can include applications that help you achieve your goals.

Your Web page can be a powerful tool in delivering service to your users, but it is only one of many tools you have. Involve students as much as possible. The main goal is to promote the library, so use the methods that work best for you.

APPENDIX A

BOOK VENDORS

Amazon Books. Online sales of books, music, videos, and so on. *www.amazon.com*

Ambassador Book Service, 42 Chasner St., Hempsted, NY 11550. 800–431–8913. *www.absbooks.com*

Anderson's Bookshop, P. O. Box 3832, Naperville, IL 60567. 800–728–0708.

Astran, Inc., 5915 S. W. 8th St., Miami, FL 33130. 305–858–4300. Wholesale books in Spanish. *www.astranbooks.com*

Baker & Taylor Co., 2709 Water Ridge Parkway, Charlotte, NC 28217. 800–775–1800. *www.btol.com*

  Eastern Division, 50 Kirby Avenue, Somerville, NJ 08876

  Midwestern Division, 501 Gladiolus St., Momence, IL 60954

  Southern Division, Mount Olive Rd., Commerce, GA 30599

  Western Divison, 380 Edison Way, Reno, NV 89564

Barnes and Noble Books. Online sales of books, music, videos, and so on. *www.barnesandnoble.com*

Bernan Associates, 4611–F Assembly Dr., Lanham, MD 20706. 800–865–3450. Government documents. *www.bernan.com*

Blackwell Publishers, 350 Main St., Malden, MA 02148. 781–388–8200. *www.blackwell.com*

Blackwell Publishers Ltd. Book Services, 108 Cowley Rd., Oxford, England OX4–1JF. 44–865–791100. British and European titles. *www.blackwell.com*

Book Depot, 1707 Ridge Rd., Lewiston, NY 14092. 800–801–7193. Out-of-print books and remainders. *www.bookdepot.com*

Book House, 208 W. Chicago St., Jonesville, MI 49250. 800–248–1146. *www.thebookhouse.com*

Book Wholesalers, 1847 Mercer Rd., Lexington, KY 40511. 800–888–4478. Books, audio, and video.

Bookmen, Inc., 525 North 3rd St., Minneapolis, MN 55401. 800–328–8411. Books, Midwest regional books. *www.bookmen.com*

Booksource, 4127 Forest Park Blvd., St. Louis, MO 63108. 800–444–0435. *www.booksource.com*

Bound To Stay Bound, Inc., 1880 West Morton Rd., Jacksonville, IL 62650. 800–637–6586. Hardbound paperbacks. *www.btsbbooks.com*

Brodart Co., 500 Arch St., Williamsport, PA 17705. 800–233–8467. *www.brodart.com*

Coutts Library Services, Inc., 1823 Maryland Ave., Niagara Falls, NY 14302. 800–772–4304. *www.coutts-ls.com*

Davidson Titles, Inc., 101 Executive Dr., P. O. Box 3538, Jackson, TN 38303–3538.

Eastern Book Co., 131 Middle St., P. O. Box 4540 DTS, Portland, ME 04112. 800–937–0331. *www.ebc.com*

Econo-Clad Books, P. O. Box 1777, Topeka, KS 66601. 800–255–3502. Hardbound paperbacks. *www.sagebrush.com/books/econoclad.cfm*

Emery-Pratt, 1966 W. Main St., Owosso, MI 48867. 800–248–3887. Books, audio, and video. *www.emerypratt.com*

Follett Library Book Co., 2233 West St., River Grove, IL 60171. 800–621–4345. *www.follett.com*

Franklin Book Co., Inc., 7804 Montogomery Ave., Elkins Park, PA 19027–2698. *www.Franklinbooks.com*

H. W. Wilson, 950 University Ave., Bronx, NY 10452. 800–367–6770. Indexes and reference materials. *www.hwwilson.com*

Hispanic Book Distributors, Inc., 240 E. Yvon Dr., Tucson, AZ 85704. 800–634–2124. *www.hispanicbooks.com*

Ingram Library Services, One Ingram Blvd., La Vergne, TN 37086. 800–937–5300. *www.ingramlibrary.com*

International Book Centre, 2391 Auburn Rd., Shelby Township, MI 48317. 810–254–7230. Foreign language books (ESL), children's and elementary materials. *www.ibcbooks.com*

James Bennett Pty. Ltd., 3 Narabang Way, Belrose NSW 2085, Australia. 62–2–9986–7000. Bookdealer for Australia and South Pacific titles. *www.blackwell.com*

Junior Library Guild, 401 E. Wilson Bridge Rd., Worthington, OH 43085. 800–743–4070. www.*juniorlibraryguild.com*

Lindsay & Howes Booksellers, Lake House, Woodside Park, Catteshall Lane, Godalming, Surrey, England GU7-1LG. 011–44–1483–425222. Books from Great Britain. *www.lindsay-howes.co.uk*

Midwest Library Service, 11443 St. Charles Rock River, Bridgeton, MO 63044. 800–325–8833. *www.midwestls.com*

Multi–Cultural Books and Videos, Inc., 28880 Southfield Road, Ste. 183, Lathrup Village, MI 48076. 800–567–2220. *www.multiculbv.com*

Nedbook International, P. O. Box 37600, 1030BA Amsterdam, The Netherlands. 31–20–6321771. Dutch and European books. *www.nedbook.nl/ NEDBOOK*

netLibrary, Inc., 3080 Center Green Dr., Boulder, CO 80301. 800–413–4557. Electronic editions of published books. *www.netlibrary.com/libraryinfo*

Penworthy Co., 219 N. Milwaukee St., Milwaukee, WI 53202. 800–265–2665.

Perfection Learning Corp., 1000 N. Second Ave., P. O. Box 500, Logan, IA 51546. 800–831–4190. *www.plconline*.com

Perma-Bound, East Vandalia Rd., Jacksonville, IL 62650. 800–637–6581. *www.perma-bound.com*

Puvill Libros, Books from Spain & Mexico, 264 Derrom Ave., Paterson, NJ 07504. 973–279–9054. *www.puvill.com*

Quality Books, Inc., 1003 West Pines Rd., Oregon, IL 61061–9680. 800–323–4241.

R. R. Bowker, 121 Chanlon Rd., New Providence, NJ 07974. 888–269–5372. *www.bookwire.bowker.com*

Regent Book Co., 25 Saddle River Rd., South Hackensack, NJ 07606; P. O. Box 750, Lodi, NJ 07644. 800–999–9554. *www.regentbook.com*

Sagebrush Corp., 12219 Nicollet Ave. South, Burnsville, MN 55337. 800–642–4648. *www.sagebrushcorp.com*

Smart Apple Media, P. O. Box 206, Mankato, MN 56002. 800–561–3943. *www.librarybooks.com*

Story House Corp., Bindery Lane, Charlotteville, NY 12036. 800–847–2105. *www.story-house.com*

World Almanac Education, 15355 NEO Parkway, Cleveland, OH 44128. 800–321–1147. *www.worldalmanac.com*

Yankee Book Peddlar, 999 Maple St., Contoocock, NH 03229. 800–258–3774. *www.ybp.com*

APPENDIX B

PERIODICAL VENDORS

B. H. Blackwell, Ltd., Beaver House, Hythe Bridge St., Oxford, England OX1 2ET. 44 (0) 1865–792792. British and European titles.

Bell & Howell Information and Learning, 300 North Zeeb Rd., P. O. Box 1346, Ann Arbor, MI 48106–1346. *www.proquest.com*

Canadian Periodical Index on CD-ROM, Gale Group, 27500 Drake Rd., Farmington Hills, MI 48331–3535. 800–877–GALE.

Congressional Information Service, Inc., 4520 East-West Highway, Suite 800, Bethesda, MD 20814–3389. 800–638–8380. *www.cipubs.com*

Demco Media, P. O. Box 14260, Madison, WI 53714–0260. 800–448–6764. *www.demcomedia.com*

EBSCO Industries, Inc., Periodical Sales Division, 5724 Highway 280 E., Birmingham, AL 35242–6818. 205–991–1369. Also located at EBSCO Subscription Services Division of EBSCO Industries, 1140 Silver Lake Rd., Cary, IL 60013–1658. 847–639–2899. *www.ebsco.com*

ERIC Document Reproduction Service, 7420 Fullerton Rd., Suite 110, Springfield, VA 22153. 800–443–3742. *http://edrs.com*

EVA Subscription Services, 290 Turnpike Rd., Suite 339, Westboro, MA 01581. 800–842–2077.

Facts on File News Services, 11 Penn Plaza, 15th Floor, New York, NY 10001. 800–363–7976. *www.facts.com*

Faxon Company, 15 Southwest Park, Westwood, MA 02090. 800–766–0039. *www.faxon.com*

G. H. Arrow Co., 2066–76 W. Hunting Park Ave., Philadelphia, PA 19140. 800–775–2776. Specializing in back issue periodicals. *www.gharrow.com*

Gale Group, 27500 Drake Rd., Farmington Hills, MI 48331–3535. 800–877–GALE. *www.galegroup.com/school*

Hawkeye Ink Back Issue Periodicals, 17435 Plainview Ave., P. O. Box 231, Redfield, SD 57469–0231. Single back issue specialists.

NewsBank, Inc., 5020 North Tamiami Trail, Suite 110, Naples, FL 34103. 800–762–8182.

Periodicals Service Co., 11 Main St., Germantown, NY 12526. 518–537–4700. *www.backsets.com*

Swets Blackwell Information Services, 440 Creamery Way, Suite A, Exton, PA 19341–2551. 800–447–9387. International library supply service provider. *www.swetsinc.com*

W. T. Cox Subscriptions, Inc., 201 Village Rd., Shallotte, NC 28470. 800–571–9554. *www.wtcox.com*

APPENDIX C

SELECTED AV PRODUCERS
AND DISTRIBUTORS

AEC One Stop Group, 23 Francis J. Clarke Circle, Bethel, CT 06801. 800–388–8889 x212. (Music) *www.aent.com*

Ambrose Video Publishing, Suite 2100, 28 West 44th St., New York, NY 10036. 800–526–4663. *www.ambrosevideo.com*

American Library Color Slide Co., Inc., Grand Central Station, P. O. Box 4414, New York, NY 10163. 800–633–3307. *www.artslides.com*

Audio Editions Books on Cassette, P. O. Box 6930, Auburn, CA 95604. 800–231–4261. *www.audioeditions.com*

Audio Visual Source, a Division of Wilmi Sales Corp., 556 Westbury Ave., Carle Place, NY 11514–0359. 800–722–0580.

AudioBound, 500 Arch St., Williamsport, PA 17705. 800–233–8467. *www.brodart.com*

Baker & Taylor, 2709 Water Ridge Parkway, Charlotte, NC 28217. 800–775–1800. *www.btol.com*

Belle Curve Records, Inc. P. O. Box 18387, Boulder, CO 80308–1387. 888–357–5867. *www.bellecurve.com*

Blackstone Audiobooks, Inc., P. O. Box 969, Ashland, OR 97520. 800–729–2665. *www.blackstoneaudio.com*

Books on Tape, Inc., P. O. Box 7900, Newport Beach, CA 92658–7900. 800–541–5525. *booksontape.com*

Children's Television Workshop, 1 Lincoln Plaza, New York, NY 10012. 212–875–6235. *www.ctw.org*

Chip Taylor Communications, 2 East View Dr., Derry, NH 03038. 800–876–CHIP.

Comex Systems, Inc., Mill Cottage, Mendham, NJ 07945. 973–543–2862 or 800–543–6959. Videotapes, study guides, library skills, basic skills materials. *www.comexsystems.com*

Coronet, See Phoenix Films, Inc.

DeBeck Educational Video, 3873 Airport Way, P. O. Box 9757, Bellingham, WA 98227–9754. 604–739–7696. *www.debeck.com*

Disney Educational Productions, 105 Terry Dr., Suite 120, Newtown, PA 18940. 800–295–5010. *www.disney.go.com/educational*

Distribution Video and Audio, 1610 N. Myrtle Ave., Clearwater, FL 33755. 800–DVA–VIDEO. *www.dva.com/library*

Educational Activities, Inc., P. O. Box 392, Freeport, NY 11520. 800–645–3739. *www.edact.com*

Educational Video Network, 1341 19th St., Huntsville, TX 77340. 800–762–0060. *www.edvidnet.com*

Encyclopaedia Britannica Educational Corp., 310 S. Michigan Ave., Chicago, IL 60604–9839. 800–747–8503.

Films for the Humanities & Sciences, P. O. Box 2053, Princeton, NJ 08543–2053. 800–257–5126. *www.films.com*

Follett Audiovisual Resources, 220 Exchange Dr., Suite A., Crystal Lake, IL 60014. 888–281–1216. *www.far.follett.com*

Guidance Associates, P. O. Box 1000, Mt. Kisco, NY 10549. 800–431–1242. *www.harb.net/guidanceassociates/*

Harris Communications, 15159 Technology Dr., Eden Prairie, MN 55344. 800–825–6758. *www.harriscomm.com*

Ingram Library Services, Inc., One Ingram Boulevard, La Vergne, TN 37086–1986. 800–937–5300. *www.ingramlibrary.com*

KC Sales, 31304 Via Colinas, Suite 103, Westlake Village, CA 91362. 800–991–8766. *www.madacyvideo.com*

L. A. Theatre Works, 681 Venice Blvd., Venice, CA 90291. 800–708–8863. *www.latheatreworks.org*

Landmark Audiobooks, 4865 Sterling Dr., Boulder, CO 80301. 800–580–2989. (Audiobook leasing) *www.landmarkaudio.com*

Library Video Co., 7 East Wynnewood Road, P. O. Box 580, Wynnewood, PA 19096. 800–843–3620. *www.libraryvideo.com*

Listening Library, an Imprint of the Random House Audio Publishing Group, 1540 Broadway, New York, NY 10036. 800–243–4504.

Live Oak Media, P. O. Box 652, Pine Plains, NY 12567. 800–788–1121

Live Wire Media, #619, 3450 Sacramento St., San Francisco, CA 94118. 800–359–KIDS. *www.livewiremedia.com*

Lucerne Media, 37 Ground Pine Rd., Morris Plains, NJ 07950. 800–341–2293.

Midwest Tape, P. O. Box 820, Holland, OH 43528. 800–875–2785. *midwesttapes.com*

MPI Home Video, 16101 South 108th Ave., Orland Park, IL 60467. 800–777–2223. *www.mpimedia.com*

Multi-Cultural Books & Videos, Inc., 28880 Southfield Road, Ste. 183, Lathrup Village, MI 48076. 800–567–2220. *www.multiculbv.com*

PBS Video, Inc., 1320 Braddock Place, Alexandria, VA 22314–1698. 800–PBS–SHOP. *www.pbs.org*

Phoenix/BFA Films & Video (Affiliate: Coronet/MTI Film & Video), 2349 Chaffee Dr., St. Louis, MO 63146. 314–569–0211 or 800–221–1274. *www.phoenix-bfa-coronet.com*

Professional Media Service Corp., 1160 Trademark Dr., Ste. 109, Reno, NV 89511. 800–223–7672. *www.btol.com*

Quality Books, Inc., A Dawson Co., 1003 West Ines Rd., Oregon, IL 61061–9680. 800–323–4241.

Rainbow Educational Media, 4540 Preslyn Dr., Raleigh, NC 27616. 800–331–4047.

Recorded Books, LLC, 270 Shipjack Rd., Prince Frederick, MD 20678–3410. 800–638–1304. *www.recordedbooks.com*

Recording for the Blind and Dyslexic, 20 Roszel Rd., Princeton, NJ 08540. 800–221–4792. (Textbooks on tape) *www.rfbd.org*

Rounder Records, One Camp St., Cambridge, MA 02140. 800–ROUNDER. *www.rounder.com*

Science Books & Films Published by the American Association for the Advancement of Science, 1200 New York Ave. NW, Washington, DC 20005. 202–326–6454.

Sign Media, Inc., 4020 Blackburn Ln., Burtonsville, MD 20866. 800–475–4756. *www.signmedia.com*

SVE/Churchill Media, 6677 North Northwest Highway, Chicago, IL 60631–1304. 800–829–1900. *www.svemedia.com*

SVS, Inc., Division of Sony Corp. of America, c/o Movies Unlimited, 1700 Broadway, 16th Floor, New York, NY 10019. 800–523–0823.

Taped Editions, Inc., #201, 4040 E. 82nd St., Suite C–9, Indianapolis, IN 46250–4209. 800–850–1701. *www.tapededitions.com*

Thomas T. Beeler, Publisher, 22 King St., P. O. Box 659, Hampton Falls, NH 03844–0659. 800–818–7574.

Time Life Education, Inc., P. O. Box 85026, Richmond, VA 23285. 800–449–2010. *www.timelifeedu.com*

Troll Communications (formerly Troll Associates), 100 Corporate Dr., Mahwah, NJ 07430. 800–541–1097. *www.troll.com*

Uproar Entertainment, 3663 Twin Lake Ridge, Westlake Village, CA 91361. 818–889–3757. (Humor)

Vide-O-GO/That's Infotainment!, P. O. Box 2994, Princeton, NJ 08543–2994. 800–323–8433. *www.videogo.com*

Video Information Source & Library DVD Source, 3395 South Jones Blvd., #212, Las Vegas, NV 89146. 702–655–5800. *www.librarydvd.com*

Video Resources Software, 11767 South Dixie Highway, Suite 222, Miami, FL 33156. 888–ACE–MATH. Specializing in Ace-tutoring products. *www.tutorace.com*

Weston Woods Studios, Inc., P.O. Box 2193, Norwalk, CT 06852–2193. 800–243–5020. *www.scholastic.com*

APPENDIX D

SOURCES FOR PURCHASING EQUIPMENT, FURNISHINGS, AND SUPPLIES

American Seating Co., 401–T American Seating Center, Grand Rapids, MI 49504. 800–748–0268. *www.americanseating.com*

ASI Sign Systems, Inc., 3890 W. Northwest Hwy., Ste. 102, Dallas, TX 75220. 800–274–7732. *www.assignsystems.com*

BC Inventar, Inc., 2216 Bissonnet St., Second Floor, Houston, TX 77005. 713–522–9715. *www.bci-usa.com*

Blanton & Moore Co., P. O. Box 70, Highway 21 South, Barium Springs, NC 28010. 704–528–4506. *www.blantonandmoore.com*

Bretford Manufacturing, Inc., 11000 Seymour Avenue, Franklin Park, IL 60131. 800–521–9614. *www.bretford.com*

Brodart Library Supplies and Furnishings, 100 North Road, Clinton County Industrial Park, McElhattan, PA 17748. 888–820–4377. *www.brodart.com*

CBA, P. O. Box 190728, Atlanta, GA 31119. 800–557–4222. *www.cbaatlanta.com*

Children's Book Council, 12 W. 37th St., 2nd Floor, New York, NY 10018. 800–999–2160. Promotional supplies. *www.cbcbooks.org*

D. B. Company, 529 Pecore, Houston, TX 77009. 877–234–1657. *www.thedbcomp.net* or *www.universalairlift.com*

Decar, division of SICO North America Inc., 96 W. Moreland Ave., Addison, IL 60101. 608–836–1911. Furniture.

DEMCO, Inc., P.O. Box 7488, Madison, WI 53707. 800–356–1200. *www.demco.com*

Display Fixtures Co., 1501 Westinghouse Blvd., P. O. Box 410073, Charlotte, NC 28241. 800–737–0880. *www.displayfixtures.com*

ENEM Systems by Harrier Interior Products Corp., 319 Colfax St., Palatine, IL 60067. 847–934–1310. *www.enembyharrier.com*

Fetzers' Inc., 1436 S. West Temple, Salt Lake City, UT 84115. 801–484–6103. *www.fetzersinc.com*

Fixture Factory, 835 NE 8th St., Gresham, OR 97030. 503–661–6525.

Fleetwood Group, Inc., P. O. Box 1259, Holland, MI 49424. 800–257–6390. *www.fleetwoodgroup.com*

Follett Library Resources, 1340 Ridgeview Drive, McHenry, IL 60050–7047. 888–511–5114. *www.titlewave.com*

Fordham Equipment & Publishing Co., 3308 Edson Ave., Bronx, NY 10469–2694. 800–249–5922. *www.bowker.com/lrg/home/entries*

Gaylord Bros., P.O. Box 4901, Syracuse, NY 13221. 800–448–6160. *www.gaylord.com*

Grafco Inc., P. O. Box 71, Catasauqua, PA 18032–0071. 800–367–6169. *www.grafco.com*

Gressco, Ltd., 328 Moravian Valley Road, P. O. Box 339, Waunakee, WI 53597. 800–345–3480. *www.gresscoltd.com*

Highsmith Company, W5227 Highway 106, Fort Atkinson, WI 53538. 800–558–2110. *www.highsmith.com*

International Library Furniture, Inc., 525 S. College, Keene, TX 76059. 888–401–0869. *www.internationallibrary.com*

J. P. Jay Associates, Inc., 1313 Roth Ave., Allentown, PA 18102. 800–969–9667.

JD Store Equipment, Inc., 136 Oregon St., El Segundo, CA 90245. 800–433–3543. *www.jdstore.com*

Jim Quinn & Associates, 1057 Leesome Lane, P. O. Box 635, Altamont, NY 12009. 888–551–1060. *http://JimQuinn.com*

Kapco Library Products, 1000 Cherry St., Kent, OH 44240. 800–791–8965. *www.kapcolibrary.com*

Kurtz Brothers, 400 Reed St., P. O. Box 392, Clearfield, PA 16830. 800–252–3811. School supplies.

Library Bureau, 172 Industrial Road, P. O. Box 400, Fitchburg, MA 01420–0004. 800–221–6638. *www.librarybureau.com*

Library Display Design Systems, P. O. Box 8143, Berlin, CT 06037. 860–828–6089.

Library Interiors Group, 2801 Division St., Metairie, LA 70002. 800–982–9909. *www.libraryinteriors.com*

Library Store, Inc., 112 E. South St., P. O. Box 964, Tremont, IL 61568. 800–548–7204. Library supplies. *www.thelibrarystore.com*

Lift Discplay, Inc., 115 River Rd., Edgewater, NJ 07020. 800–543–8269. *www.LIFTonline.com*

Midlands Co., Inc., 3640 N. Dixboro Rd., Ann Arbor, MI 48105. 734–622–0080.

Mohawk Library Furniture, 1609 Sherman Ave., Suite 312, Evanston, IL 60201. 847–570–0448.

Montel High Density Storage Systems, 225 4th Avenue, P. O. Box 130, Montmagny, QC G5V 3S5, Canada. 418–248–0235. *www.montel.com*

Neschen USA LLC, 9800 York, Wichita, KS 67215. 800–434–0293. *www.neschen.com*

Palmieri Library Furniture, 1230 Reid St., Richmond Hill, ON L4B 1C4, Canada. 800–413–4440. *www.onramp.ca/business/palmieri*

Pyramid School Products, 6510 North 54th St., Tampa, FL 33610. 800–792–2644. School and art supplies. *www.pyramidsp.com*

Ramsey Woodworks, 83 Huff Dr., Lawrenceville, GA 30044. 770–806–0656. *www.disc-display.com*

Sauder Manufacturing Co., 930 West Barre Rd., Archbold, OH 43502. 800–537–1530. *www.saudermfg.com*

School Specialty Supply, Inc., P. O. Box 1579, Appleton, WI 54913. 888–388–3224. *www.schoolspecialty.com*

Scott Machine Development Co., Route 206, P. O. Box 88, Walton, NY 13856. 800–227–2688. *www.scottmachine.com*

Stumps, One Party Place, P. O. Box 305, South Whitley, IN 46787–0305. 800–348–5084. Party supplies. *www.stumpsparty.com*

Texwood Furniture Corp., 1353 West 2nd St., Taylor, TX 76574–0431. 888–878–0000. *www.texwood.com*

Vernon Library Supplies, Inc., 2851 Cole Ct., Norcross, GA 30071. 800–878–0253. *www.vernlib.com*

Worden Co., 199 E. 17th St., Holland, MI 49423. 800–748–0561. *www.wordencompany.com*

APPENDIX E

SOURCES FOR REVIEWS OF
PRINT MATERIALS

PERIODICALS AND ANNUALLY UPDATED TOOLS

ALAN Review. National Council of Teachers of English, Assembly on Literature for Adolescents, Office of the Dean, College of Education and Human Development, Box 6960, Radford University, VA 24142. 703–831–5439. Subscriptions: 1111 Kenyon Rd., Urbana, IL 61801.

American Book Publishing Record. R. R. Bowker, P. O. Box 31, 121 Chanlon Rd., New Providence, NJ 07974.

American Music Teacher. Music Teachers National Association, Inc., 617 Vine St., Suite 1432, Cincinnati, OH 45202–2434.

Appraisal: Science Books for Young People. Children's Science Book Review Committee, 605 Commonwealth Ave., Boston, MA 02215. 617–353–4150.

Arithmetic Teacher. National Council of Teachers of Mathematics, 1906 Association Dr., Reston, VA 22091.

Book Links: Connecting Books, Libraries, and Classrooms. American Library Association, 50 E. Huron St., Chicago, IL 60611. 800-545-2433.

Book Report: The Journal for Junior and Senior High School Libraries. Linworth Publishing, 5701 North High Street, Suite One, Worthington, OH 43214. 800-798-5017.

Book Review Digest, H. W. Wilson Co., 950 University Ave., Bronx, NY 10452. 212–588–8400.

Book Review Index. Gale Research Inc., 835 Penobscot Bldg., 645 Griswold St., Detroit, MI 48226. 800–877–4253.

Bookbird. International Institute for Children's Literature and Reading Research, 138 Stanley Coulter Hall, Purdue University, W. Lafayette, IN 47907–1359. 317–494–0400.

Booklist, American Library Association, 50 E. Huron St., Chicago, IL. 60611. 800-545-2433. Twice monthly, one issue each July and August.

Books for the Teen Age. Office of Branch Libraries, New York Public Library, 455 Fifth Ave., New York, NY 10016.

Books in Canada. Canadian Review of Books Ltd., 130 Spadina Ave., Ste. 603, Toronto, ON 5V 2L4, Canada. 416–601–9880.

Books in Print. R. R. Bowker, P. O. Box 31, 121 Chanlon Rd., New Providence, NJ 07974. 800–521–8110.

Bowker Annual Library and Book Trade Almanac. R. R. Bowker, P. O. Box 31, 121 Chanlon Rd., New Providence, NJ 07974. 800–521–8110.

Braille Book Review. National Library Service for the Blind and Physically Handicapped, 1291 Taylor St. NW, Washington, DC 20542.

Bulletin of the Center for Children's Books (formerly *Center for Children's Books Bulletin*). University of Illinois Press, 54 E. Gregory Dr., Champaign, IL 61820. 217–333–0950 or 217–244–0626.

Canadian Books in Print. University of Toronto Press, 214 College St., Toronto ON M5T 3A1. 800–665–8810.

Canadian Children's Literature. University of Guelph, Department of English, Guelph, ON N1GW1, Canada.

Catholic Library World. 461 West Lancaster Ave., Haverford, PA 19041.

Changing Times. Editor's Park, MD 20782.

Children's Book Review Index. Gale Research, 835 Penobscot Bldg., 645 Griswold St., Detroit, MI 48226–4094. 313–961–2242 or 800–877–4253.

Children's Books in Print (formerly *Children's Books for Schools and Libraries*). R. R. Bowker, P. O. Box 31, 121 Chanlon Rd., New Providence, NJ 07974. 800–521–8110.

Children's Books of the Year. Bank Street College, 610 W. 112th St., New York, NY 10025.

Children's Catalog. H. W. Wilson Co., 950 University Ave., Bronx, NY 10452. 718–588–8400 or 800–367–6770.

Choice. Irving E. Rockwood, Ed., 100 Riverview Center, Middletown, CT 06457. 203–347–6933.

CM: A Reviewing Journal of Canadian Materials for Young People (formerly *CM: Canadian Materials for Schools and Libraries* and *Canadian Materials*). Canadian Library Association, CM Subscriptions, 200 Elgin St., Ste. 602, Ottawa, ON K1P 1L5, Canada. 204–945–7833.

Computing Teacher. Council for Computers in Education, 1787 Agate, University of Oregon, Eugene, OR 97403–1923.

Curriculum Review. Curriculum Advisory Service, 407 Dearborn St., Suite 1360, Chicago, IL 60605.

Electronic Learning. P. O. Box 3024, Southeast, PA 19398.

Elementary School Journal. University of Chicago Press, P. O. Box 37005, Chicago, IL 60637.

Elementary School Library Collection. Brodart Co., 500 Arch St., Williamsport, PA 17705. 800–233–8467.

El-Hi Textbooks and Serials in Print: Including Related Teaching Materials K–12. R. R. Bowker, P. O. Box 31, 121 Chanlon Rd., New Providence, NJ 07974. 800–521–8110.

Emergency Librarian. Rockland Press, Department 284, Box C34069, Seattle, WA 98124–1069.

English Journal. National Council of Teachers of English, 1111 W. Kenyon Road, Urbana, IL 61801–1086.

For Younger Readers, Braille and Talking Books. U. S. Library of Congress National Library Service for the Blind and Handicapped, 1291 Taylor St. NW, Washington, D.C. 20542. 202–707–5100.

Growing Point. Growing Point, c/o Margery Fisher, Ed., Ashton Manor, Northampton NN7 2JL, United Kingdom. 011–44–1604–862277.

History Teacher. Society for History Education, P. O. Box 1578, Borrego Springs, CA 92004. 760–767–5938.

Horn Book Magazine. Circulation Department, Park Square Building, 31 James St., Boston, MA 02116. 617–227–1555 or 800–325–1170.

Instructor (formerly *Instructor and Teacher*). Scholastic, Inc., 555 Broadway, New York, NY 10012–3999. 212–643–6100.

Interracial Books for Children Bulletin. Council on Interracial Books for Children, Box 1263, New York, NY 10023.

Journal of Youth Services In Libraries (formerly *Top of the News*). American Library Association, Association for Library Service to Children and Young Adult Library Services Association, 50 E. Huron St., Chicago, IL 60611–2795. 800-545-2433.

Junior High School Library Catalog. H. W. Wilson Co., 950 University Ave., Bronx, NY 10452. 800–367–6770.

Kirkus Reviews. Kirkus Service, 200 Park Avenue South, New York, NY 10003.

Kliatt (formerly *Kliatt Young Adult Paperback Book Guide* and *Kliatt Paperback Book Guide*). The Guide, 425 Watertown St., Newton, MA 02158. 617-237-7577.

Knowledge Quilt, School Library Media Quarterly, and *School Libraries.* American Library Association, 50 E. Huron St., Chicago, IL 60611–2795. 800–545–2433. Subscriptions: ALA, Subscription Dept., S&S Computer Services, Inc., 434 Downer Pl., Aurora, IL 60506–9936.

Language Arts. National Council of Teachers of English, 1111 Kenyon Rd., Urbana, IL 61801.

Library Journal. P. O. Box 1977, Marion, OH 43305.

Library Talk. Linworth Publishing, Inc., 5701 N. High St., Suite 1, Worthington, OH 43085. 614–436–7107 or 800–786–5017.

Multicultural Review. Greenwood Publishing Group, Inc., 88 Post Road W., Box 5007, Westport, CT 06881–5007.

New York Times Book Review. New York Times Co., Box 5792 GPO, New York, NY 10087.

Publishers Weekly. 245 W. 17th St., New York, NY 10011. 212–463–6758. Subscriptions: 800–278–2991.

Quill and Quire. Key Publishers Co. Ltd., 70 The Esplanade, 2nd Fl., Toronto, ON M5E 1R2, Canada. Subscriptions: Indas Customer Service, 35 Riviera Drive, Bldg. 17, Markham, ON L3R 8N4, Canada. 416–946–0406.

Reading Teacher. International Reading Association, P. O. Box 8137, Newark, DE 19714.

Recommended Reference Books for Small and Medium–sized Libraries. Libraries Unlimited, P. O. Box 6633, Englewood, CO 80155, 800–237–6124.

Reviewing Librarian. Ontario Library Association, 73 Richmond Street West, Toronto, ON M5H 1Z4, Canada.

School Libraries in Canada. Canadian Library Association, 200 Elgin St., Suite 602, Ottawa, ON K2P 1L5, Canada

School Library Journal. 245 W. 17th St., New York, NY 10011. 212-463-6824, 800-595-1066.

Science and Children. National Science Teachers Association, 1742 Connecticut Ave. NW, Washington, DC 20009–1171.

Science Books and Films. American Association for the Advancement of Science, 1333 H. St. NW, Washington, DC 20005.

Science Teacher. National Science Teachers Association, 1742 Connecticut Ave. NW, Washington, DC 20009.

Senior High School Library Catalog. H. W. Wilson Co., 950 University Ave., Bronx, NY 10452. 800–367–6770.

Social Education. National Council for the Social Studies, 3501 Neward St. NW, Washington, DC 20016.

Subject Guide to Children's Books in Print. See *Children's Books in Print.*

Talking Book Topics. National Library Services for the Blind and Physically Handicapped, 1291 Taylor St. NW, Washington, DC 20542.

United States Board on Books for Young People Newsletter (formerly *Friends of IBBY Newsletter*). United States Board on Books for Young People, Inc., c/o International Reading Association, 800 Barksdale Rd., Box 8139, Newark, DE 19714–8139. 302–731–1600.

U. S. Government Books. Government Printing Office, Washington, DC 20402.

University Press Books for Public and Secondary School Libraries. Association of American University Presses, 71 W. 23rd St., New York, NY 10010. 212–898–1010.

Voice of Youth Advocates. Scarecrow Press, 4720 Boston Way, Ste. A, Lanham, MD 20706–4310. 800–460–6420.

Wilson Library Bulletin. H. W. Wilson Co., 950 University Ave., Bronx, NY 10452. 718–588–8400 or 800–367–6770. (Ceased June 1995.)

ANNOTATED BIBLIOGRAPHIES

A to Zoo: Subject Access to Children's Picture Books. 5th ed. Carolyn W. Lima and John A. Lima. New York: R. R. Bowker, 1998.

Adventuring with Books. 11th ed. Ed. by Wendy K. Sutton and the Committee on the Elementary School Booklist of the National Council of Teachers of English. Urbana, Ill.: National Council of Teachers of English, 1997.

Against Border: Promoting Books for a Multicultural World. Hazel Rochman. Chicago: American Library Association, 1999.

American History for Children and Young Adults: An Annotated Bibliographic Index. Vandelia VanMeter. Englewood, Colo.: Libraries Unlimited, 1990.

American Indian Reference Books for Children and Young Adults. Barbara J. Kuipers. Englewood, Colo.: Libraries Unlimited, 1995.

Best Books for Children: Preschool Through Grade 6. 6th edition. John T. Gillespie and Corinne J. Naden. New Providence, N.J.: Reed-Elsevier, 2000.

Best Books for Junior High Readers. John T. Gillespie. New York: R. R. Bowker, 1991.

Best of Bookfinder: A Guide to Children's Literature About Interests and Concerns of Youth Ages 2–18. Sharon Spredemann Dreyer. Circle Pines, Minn.: American Guidance Services, 1992.

Best Science and Technology Reference Books for Young People. H. Robert Malinowsky. Phoenix, Ariz.: Oryx Press, 1991.

Best Years of Their Lives: A Resource Guide for Teenagers in Crisis. 2d ed. Stephanie Zvirin. Chicago: American Library Association, 1996.

Beyond Picture Books: A Guide to First Readers. Barbara Barstow and Judith Riggle. New York: R. R. Bowker, 1995.

Books for You: A Booklist for Senior High School Students. 11th ed. Leila Christenbury, ed. Urbana, Ill.: National Council of Teachers of English, 1995.

Books in Spanish for Children and Young Adults: An Annotated Guide. Series VI. Isabel Schon. Metuchen, N.J.: Scarecrow Press, 1993.

Building the Reference Collection: A How-To-Do-It Manual for School and Public Librarians. Gay Patrick. New York: Neal–Schuman, 1992.

A Child Goes Forth: A Curriculum Guide for Preschool Children. 8th ed. Barbara J. Taylor. New York: Prentice-Hall, 1998.

Children and Books. 9th ed. Zena Sutherland and Trina Schart Hyman. New York: Addison-Wesley, 1996.

Choosing Books for Children: A Commonsense Guide. 3d ed. Betsy Hearne. Urbana: University of Illinois Press, 1999.

Complete Directory of Large Print Books and Serials. New Providence, N.J.: R. R. Bowker, 2000.

Fiction for Youth: A Guide to Recommended Books. Lillian Shapiro and Barbara L. Stein. New York: Neal-Schuman, 1992.

For Reading Out Loud! A Guide to Sharing Books with Children. Margaret Mary Kimmel and Elizabeth Segal. New York: Dell Publications, 1991.

From Page to Screen: Children's and Young Adult Books on Film and Video. Joyce Moss and George Wilson, eds. Detroit: Gale Research, 1992.

Genreflecting: A Guide to Reading Interests in Genre Fiction. 4th ed. Betty Rosenberg and Diana Tixler Herald. Englewood, Colo.: Libraries Unlimited, 1995.

Guide to Popular U. S. Government Publications. 5th ed. Frank W. Hoffman and Richard Wood. Englewood, Colo.: Libraries Unlimited, 1998.

Guide to Reference Materials for School Library Media Centers. Margaret Irby Nichols. 5th ed. Englewood, Colo.: Libraries Unlimited, 1998.

High/Low Handbook: Encouraging Literacy in the 1990s. 3rd ed. Ellen V. LiBretto, comp. and ed. New York: R. R. Bowker, 1990.

Hispanic Heritage. Series IV: A Guide to Juvenile Books about Hispanic People and Cultures. Isabel Schon. Metuchen, N.J.: Scarecrow Press, 1991.

Informational Books for Children. Patricia J. Cianciolo. Chicago: American Library Association, 2000.

Juniorplots 4: A Book Talk Guide for Use with Readers Ages 12–16. John T. Gillespie and Corinne J. Naden. New Providence, N.J.: R. R. Bowker, 1992.

Kister's Best Dictionaries for Adults and Young People: A Comparative Guide. Kenneth F. Kister. Phoenix, Ariz.: Oryx Press, 1992.

Literature of Delight: A Critical Guide to Humorous Books for Children. Kimberly Olson Fakih. New York: R. R. Bowker, 1993.

Magazines for Libraries. 11th ed. Edited by Cheryl LaGuardia, Bill Katz and Linda Sternberg Katz. Providence, N.J.: R. R. Bowker, 2002.

Neal-Schuman Guide to Recommended Children's Books and Media for Use with Every Elementary Subject. Kathryn I. Matthew and Joy L. Lowe. New York: Neal-Schuman, 2002.

Picture Books for Children. 4th ed. Patricia J. Cianciolo. Chicago: American Library Association, 1997.

Play, Learn and Grow: An Annotated Guide to the Best Books and Materials for Very Young Children. James Thomas. New Providence, N.J.: R. R. Bowker, 1992.

Portraying Persons with Disabilities: An Annotated Bibliography of Fiction for Children and Teenagers. Joan Brest Friedberg, June B. Mullins, and Adelaide Weir Sukiennik. New Providence, N.J.: R. R. Bowker, 1992.

Reaching Adolescents: The Young Adult Book and the School. Arthea J. S. Reed. Macmillan, 1994.

Reading Lists for College-Bound Students. 3d ed. Doug Estell et al. New York: Arco/Prentice Hall, 2000.

Sequels: An Annotated Guide to Novels in Series. 3d ed. Janet Husband and Jonathan F. Husband. Chicago: American Library Association, 1997.

Supernatural Fiction for Teens: More Than 1300 Good Paperbacks to Read for Wonderment. 2nd ed. Cosette Kies. Englewood, Colo.: Libraries Unlimited, 1992.

Through Indian Eyes: The Native Experience in Books for Children. Beverly Slapian and Doris Seale. Philadelphia: New Society Publishers/New Society Educational Foundation, 1998.

U. S. Government Publications for the School Library Media Center. 2nd ed. Leticia T. Ekhaml and Alice J. Wittig. Englewood, Colo.: Libraries Unlimited, 1991.

World History for Children and Young Adults: An Annotated Bibliographic Index. Vandelia VanMeter. Englewood, Colo.: Libraries Unlimited, 1992.

Your Reading: A Booklist for Junior High and Middle School Students. 9th ed. C. Anne Webb, ed. Urbana, Ill.: National Council of Teachers of English, 1993.

APPENDIX F

SOURCES FOR REVIEWS OF NONPRINT MATERIALS

AV Guide. Des Plaines, Ill.: Scranton Gillette Communications. Monthly.

Best Videos for Children and Young Adults: A Core Collection for Libraries. Jennifer Jung Gallant. Santa Barbara, Calif.: ABC–Clio, 1990.

Booklist, American Library Association, 50 E. Huron St., Chicago, IL 60611. 800–545–2433. Twice monthly, one issue each July and August.

Bowker's Complete Video Directory, New Providence, N.J.: R. R. Bowker, 2000.

Children's Media Market Place. 4th ed., Barbara Stein, ed. New York: Neal-Schuman Publishers, 1995.

Curriculum Review. Chicago, Ill.: Curriculum Advisory Service. Monthly.

Digest of Software Reviews: Education. Ann Lathrop, ed. Fresno, Calif.: School and Home Courseware. Monthly.

Educational Media and Technology Yearbook. Littleton, Colo.: Libraries Unlimited. Annual.

Educational Technology. 140 Sylvan Ave., Englewood Cliffs, NJ 07632. Semimonthly.

Finding and Using Educational Videos. Barbara Stein, Gary Treadway, and Lauralee Ingram. New York: Neal-Schuman, 1998.

Guide to Selecting and Acquiring CD-ROMs, Software, and Other Electronic Publications. Stephen Bosch, Patricia Promis, and Chris Sugnet. Chicago: American Library Association, 1994.

Index to AV Producers and Distributors. 10th ed. National Information Center for Educational Media.

International Directory of Educational Audiovisuals. IDEA, NICEM, P.O. Box 8640, Albuquerque, NM 87198–8640. 505–265–3591 or 800–926–8328. Nonprofits, $320/yr; other organizations, $640/yr—single user; $1280/yr—unlimited network.

Journal of Youth Services In Libraries. American Library Association, Association for Library Service to Children, and Young Adult Library Services Association, 50 E. Huron Street, Chicago, IL 60611–2795. 800–545–2033. Quarterly.

Landers Film and Video Reviews. Landers Associates, P. O. Box 300309, Escondido, CA 92030–0309. Quarterly.

Library Hi Tech Journal. Emerald North America, 44 Brattle St., 4th Floor, Cambridge, MA 02138. 888-622-0075. Quarterly.

Library Technology Reports. Chicago: American Library Association. 800-545-2433. Bimonthly.

Mathematics Teacher. Reston, Va.: National Council of Teachers of Mathematics. Monthly.

Media and Methods. 1429 Walnut St., Philadelphia, Pa. 19102. 800-555-5657. American Society of Educators. Monthly.

Media Resources Catalog. Capitol Heights, Md.: National Archives and Records Administration, National Audiovisual Center. Annual.

Media Review Digest (Formerly *Multi Media Reviews Index*). Pierian Press, P.O. Box 1808, Ann Arbor, MI 48106. 800–678–2435. Annual.

Microform Review. Mecklermedia Corporation, 20 Ketchum Street, Westport, CT 06880. 203–226–6967 or 800–632–5537.

Online: The Magazine of Online Information Systems. Wilton, Conn.: Online, Inc. 6 times per year.

Online and CD-ROM Review. Medford, N.J.: Learned Information Inc. Bimonthly.

Only the Best: The Annual Guide to Highest-Rated Educational Software and Multimedia. Association for Supervision and Curriculum Development, 1995.

Recordings for the Blind, Catalog of Recorded Books. Princeton, N.J.: Recording for the Blind. Irregular.

School Library Journal. 245 W. 17th St., New York, NY 10011. 212-463-6024, 800-595-1066. 12 issues per year.

Schwann Spectrum. Santa Fe, N.M.: Stereophile, Inc. 4 issues per year.

Serials Review. Pierian Press, P. O. Box 1808, Ann Arbor, MI 48106. Quarterly.

Software Encyclopedia. New Providence, N.J.: R. R. Bowker. Annual.

Software Review on File. New York: Facts on File. Monthly.

Technology and Learning (formerly *Classroom Computer Learning*). Peter Li, Inc., 2451 E. River Rd., Dayton, OH 45439. 8 issues per year.

TechTrends. Washington, D.C.: Association for Educational Communications and Technology. 8 issues per year.

T.E.S.S.: The Educational Software Selector. EPIE Institute, 103–3 W. Montauk Highway, Hampton Bay, NY 11946. Annual.

Video Librarian. Randy Pitman, 2219 East View Avenue NE, Bremerton, WA 98310. Monthly.

Video Rating Guide for Libraries. Beth Blenz-Clucas, ed. Santa Barbara, Calif.: ABC-Clio. Quarterly.

Video Source Book. Syosset, N.Y.: National Video Clearinghouse. Available through Gale Research, Book Tower, Detroit, MI 48226. Annual.

APPENDIX G

FREE AND INEXPENSIVE MATERIALS

Apple Library Users Group Newsletter. Monica Ertel, Apple Computer, Inc., 10381 Bandley Dr., Cupertino, CA 95014. Free, published 4 times per year, for Apple users.

Consumer Information Catalog. Consumer Information Center–R, P. O. Box 100, Pueblo, CO 81009. 888–878–3256. Free, quarterly. Full text available free online.

Educational Shareware Library. Public domain software and shareware. *www.mm-soft.com*

Educational Software Cooperative. Membership required. *www.edu-soft.org*

Educators Grade Guide to Free Teaching Aids. Educators Progress Service, Inc., 214 Center St., Randolph, WI 53956. 414–326–3126.

Educators Guide to Free Audio and Video Materials. Educators Progress Service, Inc., 214 Center St., Randolph, WI 53956. 414–326–3126.

Educators Guide to Free Films. Educators Progress Service, Inc., 214 Center St., Randolph, WI 53956. 414–326–3126.

Educators Guide to Free Filmstrips and Slides. Educators Progress Service, Inc., 214 Center St., Randolph, WI 53956. 414–326–3126.

Educators Guide to Free Health, Physical Education & Recreation Materials. Educators Progress Service, Inc., 214 Center St., Randolph, WI 53956. 414–326–3126.

Educators Guide to Free Home Economics Materials. Educators Progress Service, Inc., 214 Center St., Randolph, WI 53956. 414–326–3126.

Educators Guide to Free Science Materials. Educators Progress Service, Inc., 214 Center St., Randolph, WI 53956. 414–326–3126.

Educators Guide to Free Social Studies Materials. Educators Progress Service, Inc., 214 Center St., Randolph, WI 53956. 414–326–3126.

Educators Guide to Guidance Materials. Educators Progress Service, Inc., 214 Center St., Randolph, WI 53956. 414–326–3126.

Educators Index of Free Materials. Educators Progress Service, Inc., 214 Center St., Randolph, WI 53956. 414–326–3126.

Educators Progress Service, Dept. Educast, 214 Center Street, Randolph, WI 53956. 888–951–4469.

Elementary Teachers Guide to Free Curriculum Materials. Educators Progress Service, Inc., 214 Center St., Randolph, WI 53956. 414–326–3126.

Federal Reserve System Public Information Catalog. Federal Reserve Bank of New York, 33 Liberty St., New York, NY 10045–0001. 212–720–6134. *app.ny.frb.org/cfpicnic/frame1.cfm*

Federal Resources for Educational Excellence. U. S. Department of Education, Office of the Deputy Secretary, 400 Maryland Ave. SW, Room 7W114, Washington, DC 20202. *www.ed.gov/free*

Free Materials for Schools and Libraries. Dyad Services, Box C34069, Dept. 284, Seattle, WA 98124–1069.

Free Resource Builder for Librarians and Teachers. 2nd ed. Comp. by Carol Smallwood. Jefferson, N.C.: McFarland, 1992.

Guide to Free Computer Materials. Educators Progress Service, Inc., 214 Center St., Randolph, WI 53956. 414–326–3126.

Subject Bibliography Index. Superintendent of Documents, Government Printing Office, Washington, DC 20402. Free subject bibliographies.

Talking Book Topics. National Library Service for the Blind and Physically Handicapped, 1291 Taylor St. NW, Washington, DC 20542. 202–707–5100 or 202–707–0744. Cassette, computer diskette, disc, electronic access, large print. Bimonthly.

U.S. Library of Congress Publications in Print. Library of Congress, 101 Independence Ave. SE, Washington, DC 20540. 202–707–5000 or 202–707–5522. General Library Information and Serials & Government Publications Division. 1993. Full text available online. Free, biennial.

Vertical File and Its Alternatives: A Handbook. Clara L. Sitter. Englewood, Colo.: Libraries Unlimited, 1992.

Vertical File Index. H. W. Wilson, 950 University Ave., Bronx, NY 10452–4224. 800–367–6770. Monthly.

ZDNet Software Library. Shareware. *www.zdnet.com/downloads/index.html*

APPENDIX H

SOURCES FOR INSTRUCTIONAL AIDS

Act II Books and Puppets, 1924 W. 10th Ave., Kennewick, WA 99336. Folkmanis puppets. *www.kidsbooksandpuppets.com*

ALA Graphics—American Library Association, 50 E. Huron St., Chicago, IL 60611. 800–545–2433. *alastore.ala.org*

Auntie Litter & U. S., Inc., P. O. Box 660128, Birmingham, AL 35266–0128. 205–967–4374. Nationally acclaimed environmental education and awareness program.

BookPage, 2143 Belcourt Ave., Nashville, TN 37212. 800–726–4242. *www.bookpage.com*

Broad Horizons, P. O. Box 450486, Garland, TX 75045. 972–234–1117. Task cards designed to encourage higher level thinking skills. *www.metronet.com/~bhorizon/broadhm.htm*

Cable in the Classroom, 1800 N. Beauregard St., Suite 100, Alexandria, VA 22311. 703–845–1400.

Constructive Playthings, 13201 Arrington Rd., Grandview, MO 64030. 800–841–6478. Educational toys, puzzles, art supplies, etc. *www. constplay.com/family/default/asp*

Cram Company, Inc., P. O. Box 426, Indianapolis, IN 46206, 301 South LaSalle St., Indianapolis, IN 46201. 800–227–4199. Globes, maps, geography links. *www.georgefcram.com*

Delta Education, 80 Northwest Blvd., P. O. Box 3000, Nashua, NH 03061. 800–258–1302. Math and science manipulatives.

Diamond School Supply. *www.diamondschoolsupply.com*

Edumart. *www.edumart.com*

Ellison Educational Equipment, Inc., 25862 Commercentre Dr., Lake Forest, CA 92630–8804. 800–253–2238. *www.ellison.com*

Folkmanis puppets online sales. *www.toykeeper.com/puppets*

JanWay Co., 11 Academy Rd., Cogan Station, PA 17728. 800–877–5242. *www.janway.com*

Kids on the Block, 9385–C Gerwig Ln., Columbia, MD 21046–1583. 410–290–9095 or 800–368–5437. Puppet programs dealing with issues such as literacy, drug abuse, child abuse, and disabilities. *www.kotb.com*

Lakeshore Learning Materials, P. O. Box 6261, Carson, CA 90749. 800–421–5354. *www.lakeshorelearning.com*

Milliken Publishing Co., 1100 Research Blvd., St. Louis, MO 63132–1700. 314-991–4220. 800–325–4136. Posters, instructional supplies. *www.millikenpub.com*

NuWay Products, 10945 E. San Salvador Dr., Scottsdale, AZ 85259. 480–661–6643. Sports coloring books. *www.tutornuway.com*

Nystrom, 3333 Elston Ave., Chicago, IL 60618. 800–621–8086. Maps, globes, social studies and geography materials. *www.nystromnet.com*

Puppetools. Puppets, teaching resources. *www.puppetools.com*

Story Teller, P. O. Box 561, Harrisburg, NC 28075. 877–FELT–FUN. ZoomStore.com Online Store. Museum models, toys, and games. *www.2alpha.com*

APPENDIX I

LISTSERVS, DISCUSSION LISTS, AND NEWSGROUPS

LISTSERVS AND DISCUSSION GROUPS

Members of listservs communicate with each other via e-mail. There can be large quantities of e-mail involved with being in a listserv. These selected sites will help you locate listservs of interest or give information on how to subscribe.

American Association of School Librarians: *www.ala.org/aasl/aasllist.html*

AASL Education of Library Media Specialists Section; AASL Independent Schools Section; AASL Supervisors Section; ICONnect Forum on Integrating Internet Resources; ICONnect Internet Technology Issues Discussion

Big 6 Skills: *www.big6.com/resources.htm*

Listserv, archives, and materials. Searchable at AskEric.

CHILDLIT-L: Children's Literature Forum: *www.tile.net/lists/childlitlchildrens.html*

ECEOL: Early Childhood Education On Line: *www.ume.maine.edu/~cofed/eceol*

ICONnect: Kids Connect: *www.ala.org/ICONN/kidsconn.html*

Homework help and referral service to K-12 students. Part of AASL's ICONnect.

LM NET: *ericir.syr.edu/lm_net*

School library media specialists communication. Searchable at AskEric.

National Council of Teachers of English: *www.ncte.org/lists* Secondary Literacy: *tile.net/listserv/secondaryliteracy.html* *Tile.net*

Helps you locate sites of interest. There are lists, vendors, and newsgroups.

Tile.net.literature listservs: *tile.net/listserv/literature.html* yalsa-l: *www.ala.org/yalsa/professional/yalsalists.html*

Young Adult Library Services Association List. From ALA.

USENET NEWSGROUPS

You can access a newsgroup site only if you are a member. Your server must be configured to access a USENET site directly.

Access will depend upon your Internet provider. From the selected sites, you will find information on how to subscribe, the mission of the newsgroups, and WWW postings for the newsgroups listed here.

rec.art.books.children: *tile.net/news/altbooks.html*
   Mission, how to join. All aspect of children's literature.

SUNETS's Index of . . . . re/arts/books: *ftp.sunet.se/pub/usenet/ rtfm.mit.edu/usenet-by-hierarchy/rec/arts/books*
   Arthurian; Holmes; Robin Hood; children's historical fiction; Tolkien; more.

Tile Net Index to K-12 Usenet Newsgroups: *tile.net/news/k12.html*
   Chat; ed; lang; library; sys.

CHAT ROOMS

Chat Room Index: *www.pwcs.edu/chat.html*
   Chat Room from Prince William County Public Schools. Room available by discipline to make it easy to chat.

Teacher's Chat: *www.realkids.com/tlchat.shtml*
   Sponsored by Real Kids/Real Adventures (com) and WebChat Broadcasting System.

Teacher Chat Room: *www.acs.ucalgary.ca/~jross/wwwboard.html*
   From University of Calgary (J. Ross); General Education. Post questions; help others; space down past application form to find topics.

PEN PALS

ePALS Classroom Exchange: *www.epals.com*
   Students in your classroom can exchange ideas and information with classrooms around the world. ePals includes 78 different countries and 64 languages.

Pen Pal Exchange: *www.iwaynet.net/~jwolve/schools.html*
   Alphabetical listing by country of schools that are seeking to exchange Pen Pal letters.

OTHER SITES

AskEric's Education Listserv Archive: *ericir.syr.edu/Virtual/ Listserv_Archives/*
   ERIC-maintained archive of listserv materials.

Children's Literature Web Guide: *www.acs.ucalgary.ca/~dkbrown/ discuss.html*
   More discussion.

Kids Chat Rooms: *falcon.jmu.edu/~ramseyil/kidchat.htm*
   From the Internet School Library Media Center Kids Site.

APPENDIX J

FILTERING SOFTWARE PACKAGES

Bess
N2H2
900 4th Avenue, Suite 3400
Seattle, WA 98164
800–971–2622
www.bess.net

Cyber Patrol
Surfcontrol, Inc.
1900 West Park Drive
Westbrough, MA 01581
800–828–2608
www.cyberpatrol.com

CyberSitter
Solid Oak Software, Inc.
P. O. Box 6826
Santa Barbara, CA 93160
www.solidoak.com/cysitter.htm

Cyber Snoop
Pearl Software, Inc.
64 East Uwchlan Avenue, Suite 230
Exton, PA 19341
800–PEARL96
www.pearlsw.com

Elron Internet Manager
Elron Software Inc., Network Management Division
7 New England Executive Park
Burlington, MA 01803
800–767–6683
www.elronsw.com/

I-Guard
Unified Research Laboratories, Inc.
1 Old Oyster Point Road
Newport News, VA 23602
757–269–2300
www.urlabs.com/public/products/product.html

The Library Channel
vImpact, Inc.
325 Meditation Lane
Columbus, OH 43235
888–542–4843
www.vimpact.net

Net Nanny
Net Nanny Software International, Inc.
15831 NE 8th, Suite 200
Bellevue, WA 98008
425–688–3008
www.netnanny.com

SmartFilter
Secure Computing
1 Almaden Boulevard, Suite 400
San Jose, CA 95113
800–692–5625
www.securecomputing.com

Surf Watch
Surfcontrol, Inc.
100 Enterprise Way, Suite 110
Scotts Valley, CA 95006
800–368–3366
www.surfcontrol.com

WebSENSE, Inc.
10240 Sorrento Valley Road
San Diego, CA 92121
800–723–1166
www.websense.com

X-Stop
Log-on Data Corporation
828 West Taft Avenue
Orange, CA 92865
888–STOP–XXX
www.xstop.com

APPENDIX K

ELECTRONIC COMMUNICATION AND DATA MANAGEMENT

ACCEPTABLE USE PLAN (AUP)

The District has adopted an Electronic Communication and Data Management Policy that states that access to the District's electronic communication and data management systems will be provided to those persons who agree to comply with this Electronic Communication and Data Management Acceptable Use Plan (AUP.) [See CQ (LOCAL)—Electronic Communication and Data Management Policy.]

AVAILABILITY OF ACCESS

Employee access to the District's system will be granted with the written approval of the immediate supervisor if the employee has met the conditions of system access.

Students will be granted access to the District's system by the system administrator or a local building designee, as appropriate. Secondary students will be assigned individual accounts. Any system user identified as a security risk or as having violated the District's Electronic Communication and Data Management Policy or AUP may be denied access to the District's system and other appropriate disciplinary action as described in the policy and regulations.

TERMINATION/ REVOCATION OF SYSTEM USER ACCOUNT

Termination of an employee's or student's access for violation of District policies or regulations will be effective on the date the principal or District coordinator receives notice of student withdrawal or revocation of system privileges, or on a future date if so specified in the notice.

OWNERSHIP OF
INTELLECTUAL
PROPERTY

No original work created by any District student or employee will be posted on a Web page under the District's control unless the District has received written consent from the student (and the student's parent) or employee who created the work.

Copyrighted software or data may not be placed on the District's electronic communication and data management systems without prior permission from the holder of the copyright and the District's Applications & Operations Department. Only the owner(s) or individual(s) the owner specifically authorizes may upload copyrighted material to the system.

System users may not redistribute copyrighted programs or data except with the prior written permission of the copyright holder or designee unless permitted by the doctrine of fair use. Such permission must be specified in the document or must be obtained directly from the copyright holder or designee in accordance with applicable copyright laws, District policy, and administrative regulations.

NOTIFICATION OF
CLAIMED
INFRINGEMENT

RISD has designated an agent to receive notifications of alleged copyright infringement. If you believe your copyrighted work is being infringed on an RISD site, please notify the Chief Information Officer.

ACCEPTABLE USE

The system may not be used for illegal purposes, in support of illegal activities, or for any other activity prohibited by District policy or guidelines.

System users will immediately notify a teacher or the system administrator if a potential security problem exists.

System users must purge electronic

mail, if applicable, in accordance with established retention guidelines.

Any display or transmission of sexually explicit images, messages, or cartoons, or any use of the electronic communications systems that contains ethnic or racial slurs or epithets, or any material that might be construed as harassing or disparaging of others on the grounds of race, national origin, sex, age, religion, or disability violates this policy and is strictly prohibited.

System users should be mindful that use of school-related electronic mail addresses might cause some recipients or other readers of that mail to assume they represent the District or school, whether or not that was the user's intention.

System users may not waste District resources related to the electronic communications system.

System users may not gain unauthorized access to resources or information.

The District expects system users to abide by the generally accepted rules of network etiquette.

Any attempt to harm or destroy District equipment or data or data of another user of the District's system, or any of the agencies or other networks that are connected to the Internet, is prohibited. Attempts to degrade or disrupt system performance are violations of District policy and administrative regulations and may constitute unlawful activity under applicable state and federal laws. Such prohibited activity includes, but is not limited to, the uploading or creating of computer viruses.

Persons whose vandalism as defined above results in system disruption or damage may be responsible for reimbursement of costs incurred, as well as other appropriate consequences. [See the Student Code of Conduct and District policies.]

Forgery or attempted forgery of electronic mail messages or misrepresentation of the identity of sender is prohibited. Attempts to read, delete, copy, or modify the electronic mail of other system users, interference with the ability of other system users to send/receive electronic mail, or the use of another person's user ID and/ or password is prohibited.

CONFIDENTIALITY OF INFORMATION

Information transmitted via the District's electronic communication and data management systems is considered confidential District information and may not be disclosed to persons other than the intended recipient without prior authorization. Users must closely monitor their system passwords. In order to maintain the integrity of the District's electronic communication and data management systems, users should not disclose their passwords to any other person. No user should attempt to gain access to another user's electronic mailbox, telephone voicemail box, computer files, or Internet account unless expressly authorized to do so by the user whose systems are being accessed, or by an authorized representative of the District. Any user who receives information such as electronic mail messages in error should not read the message, but should instead return the message to the sender. Unauthorized access or attempts to access the District's electronic communication and data management systems are strictly prohibited and will result in appropriate disciplinary action.

Students are responsible for remembering passwords.

Students may not distribute personal information about themselves or others by means of the electronic communication and data management systems.

No personally identifiable information about a District student will be posted on a Web page under the District's control unless the District has received written consent from the student's parent. An exception may be made for "directory information" as allowed by the Family Education Records Privacy Act and District Policy. [See Parental Permission Form and policies at FL.]

INFORMATION CONTENT/THIRD-PARTY SUPPLIED INFORMATION

System users knowingly introducing prohibited materials into the District's electronic communication and data management systems will be subject to suspension of access and/or revocation of privileges on the District's electronic communication and data management systems and will be subject to disciplinary action in accordance with District policies and the Student Code of Conduct.

A student who gains access to such material is expected to discontinue the access as quickly as possible and to report the incident to the supervising teacher.

PARTICIPATION IN CHAT ROOMS AND NEWSGROUPS

System users are prohibited from participating in any chat room or newsgroup accessed on the Internet through the District's electronic communication and data management systems unless authorized by the system administrator for educational or District business-related purposes.

DISCLAIMER

The District's system is provided on an "as is, as available" basis. The District does not make any warranties, whether expressed or implied, including, without limitation, those of merchantability and fitness for a particular purpose with respect to any services provided by the system and any information or software contained therein. The District does not warrant that the functions or services performed by or that the information or software contained on the system will meet the system user's requirements, or that the system will be uninterrupted or error free, or that defects will be corrected.

Opinions, advice, services, and all other information expressed by system users, information providers, service providers, or other third party individuals in the system are those of the providers and not the District.

The District will cooperate fully with local, state, or federal officials in any investigation concerning or relating to misuse of the District's electronic communication and data management systems.

Parents and guardians must be aware that while at school direct supervision is not always possible. The District will make reasonable attempts to limit access, but cannot guarantee that system users will not be able to access or create inappropriate material that is prohibited by the District's Electronic Communication and Data Management Policy. Therefore, students are expected to use the resources in a manner consistent with administrative regulations, guidelines, and user agreements and will be held responsible for their use. Additionally, parents should discuss with their children their own expectations for their child's use of electronic communications. The District expects students to follow their parents' instructions in this matter.

APPENDIX L

SELECTED PROFESSIONAL ASSOCIATIONS

American Association for the Advancement of Science, 1200 New York Ave., Washington, DC 20005. 202–326–6417. *www.aaas.org*

American Association for Vocational Instructional Materials (AAVIM), 220 Smithonia Rd., Winterville, GA 30683–9527. 800–228–4689. *www.aavim.org*

American Association of School Administrators, 1801 N. Moore St., Arlington, VA 22209. 703–528–0700. *www.aasa.org*

American Civil Liberties Union, 125 Broad St., New York, NY 10004. 212–944–9800. *www.aclu.org*

American Federation of Teachers, 555 New Jersey Ave. NW, Washington, DC 20001. 202–879–4400. *www.aft.org*

American Foundation for the Blind, 11 Penn Plaza, Ste. 300, New York, NY 10001. 800–AFB–LINE. *www.afb.org*

American Library Association, 50 E. Huron St., Chicago, IL 60611. 312–944–6780. *www.ala.org*

Association for Educational Communications & Technology, 1800 N. Stonelake Dr., Ste. 2, Bloomington, IN 47404. 812–335–7675 or 877–677–AECT. *www.aect.org*

Association for Supervision and Curriculum Development, 1703 N. Beauregard St., Alexandria, VA 22311. 800–933–ASCD. *www.ascd.org*

Association for the Advancement of Computing in Education. P. O. Box 2966, Charlottesville, VA 22902. 804–973–3987. *www.aace.org*

Canadian Library Association, 200 Elgin St., Ste. 602, Ottawa, ON K2P 1L5, Canada. 613–232–9625. *www.cla.ca*

Children's Book Council, Inc., 568 Broadway, New York, NY 10012. 212–966–1990. *www.cbcbooks.org*

Council For Exceptional Children, 1920 Association Dr., Reston, VA 22091. 800–CEC–SPED. *www.cec.sped.org*

International Reading Association, 800 Barksdale Rd., Box 8139, Newark, DE 19714. 302–731–1600. *www.reading.org*

National Association of Independent Schools, 1620 L. St. NW, Ste. 1100, Washington, DC 20036. 202–973–9700. *www.nais.org*

National Association of Professional Educators (NAPE), 412 First St. SE, Washington, DC 20003. 202–484–8969.

National Catholic Educational Association, 1077 30th St. NW, Ste. 100, Washington, DC 20007. 202–337–6232. *www.ncea.org*

National Coalition Against Censorship, 275 7th Ave., 20th Fl., New York, NY 10001. 212–807–6222. *ncac.org*

National Council for the Social Studies, 3501 Newark St. NW, Washington, DC 20016. 202–966–7840. *www.ncss.org*

National Council of Teachers of English, 1111 Kenyon Rd., Urbana, IL 61801–1096. 800–369–6283. *www.ncte.org*

National Education Association, 1201 16th St. NW, Washington, DC 20036. 202–833–4000. *www.nea.org*

National Parent-Teacher Association/National Congress of Parents and Teachers, 330 N. Wabash Ave., Ste. 2100, Chicago, IL 60611–3690. 800–307–4PTA (4782). *www.pta.org*

National Science Teachers Association, 1840 Wilson Blvd., Arlington, VA 22201–3000. 703–243–7100. *www.nsta.org*

National Storytelling Association (formerly National Association for the Preservation & Perpetuation of Storytelling), 116 1/2 W. Main St., Jonesborough, TN 37659. 423–913–8201 or 800–525–4514. *www.storynet.org*

APPENDIX M

LEARNING STYLE TYPE INDICATOR

This learning style inventory is one way to determine a student's individual style. The explanations and questions from the Web page are reprinted here. A student can log on to the Web site and take the questionnaire electronically. Then the student can go to the link that describes the characteristics of his learning type.

Learning Styles Type Indicator
By John W. Pelley, Ph.D.
Texas Tech University, Health Sciences Center, c1998
www.ttuhsc.edu/success/lsti.htm

A type indicator tells you what kind of thinking is most comfortable for you.
Type indicators are questionnaires that help you identify your own preferences for the way you process information, day-in and day-out. Thus, they describe an important part of your personality, but they don't describe all of your personality. Many aspects of personality are measured with tests and not indicators. A test measures how much of a given trait you have, such as motivation or the need for achievement. Type indicators don't measure quantitatively. They just classify you into one or the other type. Thus, you aren't a little or a lot of a type. For example, you wouldn't be a strong or a weak extravert; you would just be an extravert. If you have already taken the Myers-Briggs Type Indicator mentioned below, the score for each scale is only a measure of how certain you are of that preference. The sum total of all your preferences is your way of identifying the ways of thinking that are consistently most comfortable for you.

Most type indicators are not scientifically reliable.
The only scientifically valid instrument for determining your type is the Myers-Briggs Type Indicator® (MBTI). All other questionnaires that are called type indicators or type tests are designed to illustrate type, but are not proven to determine type accurately. If you want an unambiguous type determination, you should go to your school's counseling center and have someone who is qualified to interpret your results administer the MBTI for you.

Your type is just an expression of consistent preferences in your thinking.

As a way of developing your interest in psychological type and also to teach you something about it, I've devised a brief questionnaire that is linked below to serve as a type indicator. It is different from other type indicators in that it relies solely on your preferences in learning to determine your type. However, if you consider that learning is just another form of thinking, just as shopping for a car or deciding on a career, then you can conclude that your type preferences in learning are the same as your type preferences in general.

If you aren't sure what your preferences are, you might bias your type.

Before you proceed with the type questionnaire, I need to give you a caution about bias in determining your type. You will notice that all of the questions are "forced choice," meaning you choose one of two opposites. That is because, by definition, if you prefer one you cannot simultaneously prefer the other. The mistake most first-timers make in thinking about type is the assumption that being a type is saying you think only that one way. Just remember that having a preference in your thinking does not prevent you from thinking the opposite way. A classic case is the question that makes you choose between head and heart. When I first encountered this question about my psychological type, I thought, "OK, I'm usually pretty logical, but I have strong feelings, too. So I'm both." Well, I was wrong. What I didn't see at the time was that it is OK to be logical and still have feelings. It makes it a little clearer when you look at it this way. The question is really asking what do you trust the most to make your decisions? That makes it much easier for me, because I know I don't trust my feelings. I much prefer to use logic. It is interesting to note that since I became knowledgeable in the area of psychological type (I was qualified by the Association for Psychological Type in 1986), I now have learned to consider feelings as additional facts to incorporate into my logic. This is very different from people who use primarily feelings, values, and human outcomes as the basis for their decisions and who are uncomfortable in trusting their use of logic.

The way you think at work (or school) isn't necessarily an indication of your type.

A second way you can bias your type determination is to confuse what you do at work with what you actually prefer to do. A pediatric resident came up to me after a workshop and pointed to his appointment book to show me how his day was structured and planned out. He told me that my description of the perceptive type, that is adaptive and flexible, describes him best, but since he is so structured at work he seems to be the opposite type. I asked him if he used the appointment book when he went home and he told me no, at home he could do as he wanted. You see, if he were the organized judging type, he would have *wanted* to use it at home too.

Type summaries can help you sort out uncertainties in determining your type.
Now you know that you can unwittingly bias your type. You always need to compare your results with a reliable description of your type to confirm that it sounds like you. I guarantee you, only one of the 16 types will sound uniquely like you. You can get an inexpensive description of the types from CAPT, Inc. The book *Looking at Type: The Fundamentals* by Charles Martin, Ph.D. (Product No. 60107) will provide you with in-depth descriptions of each of the types. Type summaries are also available in Appendix A of *SuccessTypes for Medical Students* for those of you who already have it. I wouldn't trust the type descriptions available on the Web unless the contributing individual is a member of the Association for Psychological Type.

Now let's go to the Learning Style Type Indicator
Additional type descriptions are also available in the publication *Introduction to Type* TM (5th ed.) from CAPT, Inc. 800-777-2278 (Prod. No. 30022). The type descriptions in this booklet are more thorough and may help you find the "real" you. The Success Types book can also be obtained from CAPT, Inc. (Prod. No. 60127).

The Success Types Learning Style Type Indicator
by John W. Pelley, Ph.D.
Texas Tech University, Health Sciences Center, c1998
www.ttuhsc.edu/success/lsti.htm

Each of the questions or statements below represent opposites in your thinking when you are learning[1]. Choose the one that describes the way you really are. It is common to want to choose the one that represents what you want to be or what others think you ought to be. Try to imagine that you are learning for yourself and not for a teacher and that there is no grade involved. For example, you are learning about something that interests you like a new hobby or outside interest. Just enter the boldface letter of your choice in the box to the left, so that you can total them when you are done.

Choose the description that best fits you.					
1. ☐	E	I study best with other people.	I	I study best by myself.
2. ☐	E	When I study with other people, I get the most out of expressing my thoughts.	I	When I study with other people, I get the most out of listening to what others have to say.
3. ☐	E	When I study with other people, I get the most out of quick, trial-and-error thinking.	I	When I study with other people, I get the most out of thinking things through before I say them.
4. ☐	E	I prefer to start my learning by doing something active and then considering the results later.	I	I prefer to start my learning by considering something thoroughly and then doing something active with it later.
5. ☐	E	I need frequent breaks when I study and interruptions don't bother me.	I	I can study for very long stretches and interruptions are not welcome.
6. ☐	E	I prefer to demonstrate what I know.	I	I prefer to describe what I know.
7. ☐	E	I like to know what other people expect of me.	I	I like to set my own standards for my learning.
8. ☐	S	I am more patient with routine or details in my study.	N	I am more patient with abstract or complex material.
9. ☐	S	I am very uncomfortable with errors of fact.	N	I consider errors of fact to be another useful way to learn.
10. ☐	S	I am very uncomfortable when part of my learning is left to my imagination.	N	I am bored when everything I am supposed to learn is presented explicitly.
11. ☐	S	I prefer to learn fewer skills and get really good at them.	N	I prefer to keep learning new skills and I'll get good at them when I have to.
12. ☐	S	I learn much better in a hands-on situation to see what-is.	N	I learn much better when I'm thinking about the possibilities to imagine what might be.
13. ☐	S	I prefer to learn things that are useful and based on established principles.	N	I prefer to learn things that are original and stimulate my imagination.
14. ☐	S	I always re-examine my answers on test questions just to be sure.	N	I usually trust my first hunches about test questions.

15. ☐	S	I emphasize observation over imagination.	N	I emphasize imagination over observation.
16. ☐	S	I'm more comfortable when the professor sticks closely to the handout.	N	I'm likely to get bored if the professor sticks closely to the handout.
17. ☐	T	I prefer to have a logical reason for what I learn.	F	I prefer to see the human consequences of what I learn.
18. ☐	T	I prefer a logically organized teacher to a personable teacher.	F	I prefer a personable teacher to a logically organized teacher.
19. ☐	T	I prefer group study as a way to give and receive critical analysis.	F	I prefer group study to be harmonious.
20. ☐	T	I prefer to study first what should be learned first.	F	I prefer to study first what appeals to me the most.
21. ☐	T	The best way to correct a study partner is to be blunt and direct.	F	The best way to correct a study partner is to be tactful and understanding.
22. ☐	J	I prefer to study in a steady, orderly fashion.	P	I prefer to study in a flexible, even impulsive, way.
23. ☐	J	I stay on schedule when I study regardless of how interesting the assignment is.	P	I tend to postpone uninteresting or unpleasant assignments.
24. ☐	J	I tend to be an over-achiever in my learning.	P	I tend to be an under-achiever in my learning.
25. ☐	J	I prefer to structure my study now to avoid emergencies later.	P	I prefer to stay flexible in my study and deal with emergencies when they arise.
26. ☐	J	I prefer to give answers based on the information I already have.	P	I prefer to seek more information before deciding on an answer.
27. ☐	J	I prefer to finish one assignment before starting another one.	P	I prefer to have several assignments going at once.
28. ☐	J	I like well-defined learning assignments.	P	I like learning from open-ended problem solving.

Let's boil it down to four letters: E or I ☐ Record the letter that occurred the most for questions 1–7.

S or N ☐ Record the letter that occurred the most for questions 8–16.

T ☐
or
F
J ☐
or
P

Record the letter that
occurred the most for
questions 17–21.
Record the letter that
occurred the most for
questions 22–28.

Now arrange the letters starting
at the top, from left to right.
Based on the choices you made
above, the four letter combination
to the right could represent your type.

E or I **S or N** **T or F** **J or P**

☐   ☐   ☐   ☐

[1] This questionnaire was adapted from Table 5.1 in *SuccessTypes for Medical Students*, J. W. Pelley and B. K. Dalley (Texas Tech Univ. Extended Learning, 1997) and, with permission, from the table on learning preferences in *People Types and Tiger Stripes* (3rd ed., pp. 43–46) by Gordon D. Lawrence, 1995. Gainesville, FL; Center for Applications of Psychological Type.

APPENDIX N

LIBRARY BILL OF RIGHTS

The American Library Association affirms that all libraries are forums for information and ideas, and that the following basic policies should guide their services.

I. Books and other library resources should be provided for the interest, information, and enlightenment of all people of the community the library serves. Materials should not be excluded because of the origin, background, or views of those contributing to their creation.

II. Libraries should provide materials and information presenting all points of view on current and historical issues. Materials should not be proscribed or removed because of partisan or doctrinal disapproval.

III. Libraries should challenge censorship in the fulfillment of their responsibility to provide information and enlightenment.

IV. Libraries should cooperate with all persons and groups concerned with resisting abridgment of free expression and free access to ideas.

V. A person's right to use a library should not be denied or abridged because of origin, age, background, or views.

VI. Libraries which make exhibit spaces and meeting rooms available to the public they serve should make such facilities available on an equitable basis, regardless of the beliefs or affiliations of individuals or groups requesting their use.

Adopted June 18, 1948.
Amended February 2, 1961, and January 23, 1980, inclusion of "age" reaffirmed January 23, 1996, by the ALA Council.
Reprinted with permission of the American Library Association

ACCESS TO RESOURCES AND SERVICES IN THE SCHOOL LIBRARY MEDIA PROGRAM: AN INTERPRETATION OF THE LIBRARY BILL OF RIGHTS

The school library media program plays a unique role in promoting intellectual freedom. It serves as a point of voluntary access to information and ideas and as a learning laboratory for students as they acquire critical thinking and problem solving skills needed in a pluralistic society. Although the educational level and program of the school necessarily shapes the resources and services of a school library media program, the principles of the Library Bill of Rights apply equally to all libraries, including school library media programs.

School library media professionals assume a leadership role in promoting the principles of intellectual freedom within the school by providing resources and services that create and sustain an atmosphere of free inquiry. School library media professionals work closely with teachers to integrate instructional activities in classroom units designed to equip students to locate, evaluate, and use a broad range of ideas effectively. Through resources, programming, and educational processes, students and teachers experience the free and robust debate characteristic of a democratic society.

School library media professionals cooperate with other individuals in building collections of resources appropriate to the developmental and maturity levels of students. These collections provide resources which support the curriculum and are consistent with the philosophy, goals, and objectives of the school district. Resources in school library media collections represent diverse points of view on current as well as historical issues.

While English is, by history and tradition, the customary language of the United States, the languages in use in any given community may vary. Schools serving communities in which other languages are used make efforts to accommodate the needs of students for whom English is a second language. To support these efforts, and to ensure equal access to resources and services, the school library media program provides resources which reflect the linguistic pluralism of the community.

Members of the school community involved in the collection development process employ educational criteria to select resources unfettered by their personal, political, social, or religious views. Students and educators served by the school library media program have access to resources and services free of constraints resulting from personal, partisan, or doctrinal disapproval. School library media professionals resist efforts by individuals or groups to define what is appropriate for all students or teachers to read, view, hear, or access via electronic means.

Major barriers between students and resources include but are not limited to: imposing age or grade level restrictions on the use of resources, limiting the use of interlibrary loan and access to electronic information, charging fees for information in specific formats, requiring permission from parents or teachers, establishing restricted shelves or closed collections, and labeling. Policies, procedures, and rules related to the use of resources and services support free and open access to information.

The school board adopts policies that guarantee students access to a broad range of ideas. These include policies on collection development and procedures for the review of resources about which concerns have been raised. Such policies, developed by persons in the school community, provide for a timely and fair hearing and assure that procedures are applied equitably to all expressions of concern. School library media professionals implement district policies and procedures in the school.

Adopted July 2, 1986; amended January 10, 1990; July 12, 2000, by the ALA Council.
Reprinted with permission of the American Library Association

CHALLENGED MATERIALS: AN INTERPRETATION OF THE LIBRARY BILL OF RIGHTS

The American Library Association declares as a matter of firm principle that it is the responsibility of every library to have a clearly defined materials selection policy in written form which reflects the Library Bill of Rights, and which is approved by the appropriate governing authority.

Challenged materials which meet the criteria for selection in the materials selection policy of the library should not be removed under any legal or extra-legal pressure. The Library Bill of Rights states in Article I that "Materials should not be excluded because of the origin, background, or views of those contributing to their creation," and in Article II, that "Materials should not be proscribed or removed because of partisan or doctrinal disapproval." Freedom of expression is protected by the Constitution of the United States, but constitutionally protected expression is often separated from unprotected expression only by a dim and uncertain line. The Constitution requires a procedure designed to focus searchingly on challenged expression before it can be suppressed. An adversary hearing is a part of this procedure.

Therefore, any attempt, be it legal or extra-legal, to regulate or suppress materials in libraries must be closely scrutinized to the end that protected expression is not abridged.

Adopted June 25, 1971; amended July 1, 1981; amended January 10, 1990, by the ALA Council.
Reprinted with permission of the American Library Association

THE FREEDOM TO READ STATEMENT

The freedom to read is essential to our democracy. It is continuously under attack. Private groups and public authorities in various parts of the country are working to remove or limit access to reading materials, to censor content in schools, to label "controversial" views, to distribute lists of "objectionable" books or authors, and to purge libraries. These actions apparently rise from a view that our national tradition of free expression is no longer valid; that censorship and suppression are needed to avoid the subversion of politics and the corruption of morals. We, as citizens devoted to reading and as librarians and publishers responsible for disseminating ideas, wish to assert the public interest in the preservation of the freedom to read.

Most attempts at suppression rest on a denial of the fundamental premise of democracy: that the ordinary citizen, by exercising critical judgment, will accept the good and reject the bad. The censors, public and private, assume that they should determine what is good and what is bad for their fellow citizens.

We trust Americans to recognize propaganda and misinformation, and to make their own decisions about what they read and believe. We do not believe they need the help of censors to assist them in this task. We do not believe they are prepared to sacrifice their heritage of a free press in order to be "protected" against what others think may be bad for them. We believe they still favor free enterprise in ideas and expression.

These efforts at suppression are related to a larger pattern of pressures being brought against education, the press, art and images, films, broadcast media, and the Internet. The problem is not only one of actual censorship. The shadow of fear cast by these pressures leads, we suspect, to an even larger voluntary curtailment of expression by those who seek to avoid controversy.

Such pressure toward conformity is perhaps natural to a time of accelerated change. And yet suppression is never more dangerous than in such a time of social tension. Freedom has given the United States the elasticity to endure strain. Freedom keeps open the path of novel and creative solutions, and enables change to come by choice. Every silencing of a heresy, every enforcement of an orthodoxy, diminishes the toughness and resilience of our society and leaves it the less able to deal with controversy and difference.

Now as always in our history, reading is among our greatest freedoms. The freedom to read and write is almost the only means for making generally available ideas or manners of expression that can initially command only a small audience. The written word is the natural medium for the new idea and the untried voice from which come the original contributions to social growth. It is essential to the extended discussion that serious thought requires, and to the accumulation of knowledge and ideas into organized collections.

We believe that free communication is essential to the preservation of a free society and a creative culture. We believe that these pressures toward conformity present the danger of limiting the range and variety of inquiry and expression on which our democracy and our culture depend. We believe that every American community must jealously guard the freedom to publish and to circulate, in order to preserve its own freedom to read. We believe that publishers and librarians have a profound responsibility to give validity to that freedom to read by making it possible for the readers to choose freely from a variety of offerings. The freedom to read is guaranteed by the Constitution. Those with faith in free people will stand firm on these constitutional guarantees of essential rights and will exercise the responsibilities that accompany these rights.

We therefore affirm these propositions:

1. It is in the public interest for publishers and librarians to make available the widest diversity of views and expressions, including those that are unorthodox or unpopular with the majority.

   Creative thought is by definition new, and what is new is different. The bearer of every new thought is a rebel until that idea is refined and tested. Totalitarian systems attempt to maintain themselves in power by the ruthless suppression of any concept that challenges the established orthodoxy. The power of a democratic system to adapt to change is vastly strengthened by the freedom of its citizens to choose widely from among conflicting opinions offered freely to them. To stifle every nonconformist idea at birth would mark the end of the democratic process. Furthermore, only through the constant activity of weighing and selecting can the democratic mind attain the strength demanded by times like these. We need to know not only what we believe but why we believe it.

2. Publishers, librarians, and booksellers do not need to endorse every idea or presentation they make available. It would conflict with the public interest for them to establish their own political, moral, or aesthetic views as a standard for determining what should be published or circulated.

   Publishers and librarians serve the educational process by helping to make available knowledge and ideas required for the growth of the mind and the increase of learning. They do not foster education by imposing as mentors the patterns of their own thought. The people should have the freedom to read and consider a broader range of ideas than those that may be held by any single librarian or publisher or government or church. It is wrong that what one can read should be confined to what another thinks proper.

3. It is contrary to the public interest for publishers or librarians to bar access to writings on the basis of the personal history or political affiliations of the author.

    No art or literature can flourish if it is to be measured by the political views or private lives of its creators. No society of free people can flourish that draws up lists of writers to whom it will not listen, whatever they may have to say.

4. There is no place in our society for efforts to coerce the taste of others, to confine adults to the reading matter deemed suitable for adolescents, or to inhibit the efforts of writers to achieve artistic expression.

    To some, much of modern expression is shocking. But is not much of life itself shocking? We cut off literature at the source if we prevent writers from dealing with the stuff of life. Parents and teachers have a responsibility to prepare the young to meet the diversity of experiences in life to which they will be exposed, as they have a responsibility to help them learn to think critically for themselves. These are affirmative responsibilities, not to be discharged simply by preventing them from reading works for which they are not yet prepared. In these matters values differ, and values cannot be legislated; nor can machinery be devised that will suit the demands of one group without limiting the freedom of others.

5. It is not in the public interest to force a reader to accept with any expression the prejudgment of a label characterizing it or its author as subversive or dangerous.

    The ideal of labeling presupposes the existence of individuals or groups with wisdom to determine by authority what is good or bad for the citizen. It presupposes that individuals must be directed in making up their minds about the ideas they examine. But Americans do not need others to do their thinking for them.

6. It is the responsibility of publishers and librarians, as guardians of the people's freedom to read, to contest encroachments upon that freedom by individuals or groups seeking to impose their own standards or tastes upon the community at large.

    It is inevitable in the give and take of the democratic process that the political, the moral, or the aesthetic concepts of an individual or group will occasionally collide with those of another individual or group. In a free society individuals are free to determine for themselves what they wish to read, and each group is free to determine what it will recommend to its freely associated members. But no group has the right to take the law into its own hands, and to impose its own concept of politics or morality upon other members of a democratic society. Freedom is no freedom if it is accorded only to the accepted and the inoffensive.

7. It is the responsibility of publishers and librarians to give full meaning to the freedom to read by providing books that enrich the quality and diversity of thought and expression. By the exercise of this affirmative responsibility, they can demonstrate that the answer to a "bad" book is a good one, the answer to a "bad" idea is a good one.

    The freedom to read is of little consequence when the reader cannot obtain matter fit for that reader's purpose. What is needed is not only the absence of restraint, but the positive provision of opportunity for the people to read the best that has been thought and said. Books are the major channel by which the intellectual inheritance is handed down, and the principal means of its testing and growth. The defense of the freedom to read requires of all publishers and librarians the utmost of their faculties, and deserves of all citizens the fullest of their support.

We state these propositions neither lightly nor as easy generalizations. We here stake out a lofty claim for the value of the written word. We do so because we believe that it is possessed of enormous variety and usefulness, worthy of cherishing and keeping free. We realize that the application of these propositions may mean the dissemination of ideas and manners of expression that are repugnant to many persons. We do not state these propositions in the comfortable belief that what people read is unimportant. We believe rather that what people read is deeply important; that ideas can be dangerous; but that the suppression of ideas is fatal to a democratic society. Freedom itself is a dangerous way of life, but it is ours.

This statement was originally issued in May of 1953 by the Westchester Conference of the American Library Association and the American Book Publishers Council, which in 1970 consolidated with the American Educational Publishers Institute to become the Association of American Publishers.

Adopted June 25, 1953; revised January 28, 1972, January 16, 1991, July 12, 2000, by the ALA Council and the AAP Freedom to Read Committee.
A Joint Statement by: American Library Association and Association of American Publishers

THE FREEDOM TO VIEW STATEMENT

The FREEDOM TO VIEW, along with the freedom to speak, to hear, and to read, is protected by the First Amendment to the Constitution of the United States. In a free society, there is no place for censorship of any medium of expression. Therefore these principles are affirmed:

1. To provide the broadest access to film, video, and other audiovisual materials because they are a means for the communication of ideas. Liberty of circulation is essential to insure the constitutional guarantees of freedom of expression.
2. To protect the confidentiality of all individuals and institutions using film, video, and other audiovisual materials.
3. To provide film, video, and other audiovisual materials which represent a diversity of views and expression. Selection of a work does not constitute or imply agreement with or approval of the content.
4. To provide a diversity of viewpoints without the constraint of labeling or prejudging film, video, or other audiovisual materials on the basis of the moral, religious, or political beliefs of the producer or filmmaker or on the basis of controversial content.
5. To contest vigorously, by all lawful means, every encroachment upon the public's freedom to view.

This statement was originally drafted by the Freedom to View Committee of the American Film and Video Association (formerly the Educational Film Library Association) and was adopted by the AFVA Board of Directors in February 1979. This statement was updated and approved by the AFVA Board of Directors in 1989.
Endorsed by the ALA Council January 10, 1990
Reprinted with permission of the American Library Association

INDEX

ABOUT THE AUTHORS

BARBARA L. STEIN

Barbara L. Stein is a Professor at the University of North Texas School of Library and Information Sciences where she teaches in an online school library certification program. She has worked as a school librarian in elementary, middle, and high schools.

RISA W. BROWN

Risa W. Brown is the Library Media Specialist at Lake Highlands High School in Dallas, Texas. She has library experience in elementary and high schools, as well as public and academic libraries.